KT-225-354

Contents

Stinky

Stinky

What do you call a smelly time traveller?

Doctor Poo!

What is the smelliest instrument in a brass band?

A trump-et!

What smells and sounds like a bell?

Dung!

All the toilets have been stolen from the police station...

... they have nothing to go on!

Published in 2011
by Igloo Books Ltd
Cottage Farm
Sywell
NN6 0BJ
www.igloo-books.com

Copyright © 2011 Igloo Books Ltd

C005 0711

2 4 6 8 10 9 7 5 3 1

ISBN: 978-0-85734-716-9

Printed and manufactured in China

Stinky

What do you call a flying skunk?

A smelli-copter!

What do you call a fairy who doesn't take a bath?

Stinker-bell!

Did you hear the joke about the fart?

It stinks!

Thomas: "Mum, please can I lick the bowl?"

Mum: "No! Flush it like everyone else!"

Why did Jason take his own toilet roll to the birthday party?

Because he was a party pooper!

What did the mouth say to the eye?

"Something between us smells!"

What are two robbers called?

A pair of nickers!

Why did Tigger have his head down the toilet?

Because he was looking for Pooh!

Stinky

What did one toilet say to the other one?

"You look flushed!"

What did the boy fly say to the girl fly?

"Is this stool taken?"

Richard was walking down the street when he slipped on a pile of sick. He got up and started to walk away. He heard a yelp, behind him. Phillippa had slipped on the pile of stinky sick, too. He turned around, laughed and said, "I've just done that!" Phillippa was not impressed, "Well you could have cleaned it up!" she said.

What's brown and sticky?

A brown stick!

Stinky

What do you call a goblin with a twisted ankle?

A hoblin goblin!

What do you call an ancient Egyptian ruler with no teeth?

A gummy mummy!

What's a hanky used for?

Cold storage!

What do nappies and garbage trucks have in common?

They both hold a smelly load!

10

Stinky

Knock, knock.

Who's there!

Colleen!

Colleen who?

Colleen up this mess!

What did the sailor see in the toilet?

The captain's log!

What do you call an Igloo without a toilet?

Ig!

What do you call a newborn skunk?

A little stinker!

Stinky

What do you call a man who forgets to put his pants on?

Nicholas!

What flower is tall and smells?

A giraf-odill!

Knock, knock.
Who's there?
Smell mop.
Smell mop who?
Erm, no thanks!

How do you make a toilet roll?

Throw it down a hill!

Stinky

Boys are so dirty, the only time they wash their ears is when they eat a watermelon!

What happened when the dinosaur ate some brussel sprouts?

It did a jurassic fart!

Why does Tigger smell so bad?

Because he plays with Pooh all day!

What happens when you play table tennis with a bad egg?

First it goes ping, then it goes pong!

What do you call a huge, hairy, stinky beast?

King Pong!

Stinky

What did the shoe say to the foot?

"This job really stinks!"

What did the submarine say to the ship?

"I can see your bottom!"

What tree can't you climb?

A lavatory!

What do you call an elephant that never washes?

A smelly-phant!

Stinky

What do you get if you cross a Scottish monster with a bad egg?

The Loch Ness Pongster!

What do you call a woman with a toilet on her head?

Lou!

What do you get if you cross a worm with a toad?

A boy!

What do you get if you cross a skunk with a bear?

Winnie the Pooh!

Stinky

What famous artist had one toilet upstairs and one downstairs?
Two-loos Lautrec!

What's green and smelly?
The Hulk farting!

How does a skunk call home?
On his smell-phone!

What do you call a woman with two toilets on her head?
Lulu!

Stinky

My brother is built upside down...

... his nose runs and his feet smell!

What do you get if you cross martial arts with a deadly fart?

Kung Poo!

What's the smelliest city in America?

Poo York!

Why did the snooker player use the toilet?

He needed to pot the brown!

Why do traffic lights go red?

Well you would go red if you had to stop and go in the middle of the road!

Stinky

Did you hear about the boy who put on a clean pair of socks every day?

By the end of the week he couldn't get his shoes on!

Why did the toilet roll down the hill?

To get to the bottom!

What gets wet as it dries?

A towel!

What's it called when you ignore a bad toilet?

Evil-loo-shun!

Stinky

Knock, knock.

Who's there?

Worzel.

Worzel who?

It's upstairs, first on the left!

What do flies and stinky feet have in common?

You can shoe them, but they never go away!

What's the smelliest hair style?

Pigtails!

Knock, knock.

Who's there?

Luke.

Luke who?

Luke out, here comes a big fart!

What do you get if you cross a boomerang with a skunk?

A stink you can't get rid of!

How do poos greet one another?

How do you do-do?

How do you define agony?

A one-armed man hanging from a cliff with an itchy bum!

What's the difference between a toilet brush and a biscuit?

Dunk them in your tea and you'll soon find out!

Stinky

What did one toilet roll say to the other?

"People keep ripping me off!"

When is underwear like flowers in the garden?

When it's a pair of pink bloomers!

Why do boys have spots?

So they can play dot-to-dot!

What do you get if you cross a birthday cake and brussel sprouts?

A cake that blows out its own candles!

How do monsters begin fairy tales?

Once upon a slime!

What's the difference between a musician and a corpse?

One composes and the other decomposes!

What's long, rotten and smells of cheese?

Your toenails!

Knock, knock.
Who's there?
Danielle.
Danielle who?
Danielle at me, it was the dog!

What's the difference between a skunk and a boy?

Not much!

22

Knock, knock.

Who's there?

Jam!

Jam who?

Jam mind, I'd like some privacy in here!

What has a broom and flies?

A janitor covered in poo!

Did you ever see the movie 'Constipated'?

It never came out!

Knock, knock.

Who's there?

Hallie.

Hallie who?

Hallie-tosis, your breath stinks!

23

What do you get if you cross a skunk with a dinosaur?

A stinka-saurus!

What do stinky boys wear?

Dung-garees!

Why did the man put his eye in the freezer?

He wanted to make an eye-cicle!

What happened to the thief who stole a ton of prunes?

He was on the run for weeks!

Stinky

Knock, knock.
Who's there?
Armageddon.
Armageddon who?
Armageddon out of here, it stinks!

Who is green and eats porridge?
Mouldy Locks!

What's frozen water?
Ice.
What's frozen cream?
Ice-cream.
What's frozen tea?
Iced tea.
What's frozen ink?
Iced ink.
Phew, you do – go take a shower!

Why did the man eat ten tins of baked beans?
He wanted to go windsurfing!

Stinky

Knock, knock.
Who's there?
Nicholas.
Nicholas who?
Nicholas girls shouldn't climb trees!

They say **ignorance is bliss. That's why boys are always so happy!**

What books do skunks like to read?
Best-smellers!

Knock, knock.
Who's there?
Sarah.
Sarah who?
Sarah bad smell in the room?

26

What did the judge say when the silent but deadly fart was on trial?

"Odour in court!"

How do you cope with a gas leak?

Send the person out of the room and open the window!

Why did the fish smell so bad?

Long time, no sea!

Do you want to hear some more fart jokes?

No, they really stink!

Stinky

Did you hear about the giant that threw up?

It was all over town!

Patient: "Doctor, doctor, my husband smells like a fish."

Doctor: "Poor sole!"

What do you call a skunk who's won the lottery?

Stinking rich!

Knock, knock.

Who's there?

Mustapha.

Mustapha who?

Mustapha wee before I wet myself!

Stinky

Why did the girl kiss the boy?

To see if he would turn into a toad!

How do you get a tissue to dance?

Put a boogie into it!

What do you call little piles of rubbish?

Dumplings!

Matt is so lazy that he sticks his nose out of the window, so that the wind will blow it for him!

Did you hear about the horrid monster's farmyard impressions?

He didn't make the noises, just the smells!

Stinky

What is the feeling that you've smelled a certain fart before called?

Deja-phew!

Does an owl get embarrassed when it farts?

No, it doesn't give a hoot!

What's the worst thing that can happen to a bat while it's sleeping?

Diarrhea!

What's found at the South Pole and smells?

A ponguin!

Knock, knock.

Who's there?

Donut.

Donut who?

Donut go in the bathroom, it stinks in there!

What kind of trees do Plumbers plant?

Toiletries!

What do you get if you cross a skunk and a balloon?

A creature that stinks to high heaven!

What's yellow and smalls of dead people?

Cannibal puke!

Stinky

Knock, knock.

Who's there?

Ivy.

Ivy who?

Ivy really itchy bum!

Why is it not pleasant to kiss a vampire?

They have bat breath!

What do you call a flag in a toilet?

Bog standard!

Knock, knock.

Who's there?

Harriet.

Harriet who?

Harriet up in there!

Stinky

What do you call an aunt who falls off the toilet?

Lou Roll!

What do you get if you cross a cartoon penguin and a fart?

Pingu Pong!

Knock, knock.

Who's there?

Alec.

Alec who?

Alec to pick my nose!

How are farts able to avoid danger?

By using their in-stinks and common-scents!

Tom: "What's the difference between bogies and chocolate?"

Josh: "I don't know!"

Tom: "Well I'm never sending you out to the shops for me!"

School

What instrument did the skeleton play in the school orchestra?

A trom-bone!

What happened to the naughty little witch at school?

She was ex-spelled!

What language does a billboard speak?

Sign language!

What's the difference between school dinners and a pile of worms?

School dinners are on plates!

Teacher: "What would you do if I came to school with a face as dirty as yours?"

Pupil: "Nothing, Miss, I'm far too polite!"

What did the ghost teacher say to his class?

Don't spook until you're spooken to!

What's the most important thing to remember in chemistry?

Never, ever, lick the spoon!

Teacher: "Here's a percentage question. If there are ten questions and you get ten correct, what do you get?"

Pupil: "Accused of cheating!"

What's tall, orange, wears glasses and carries a pile of books?

A carrot disguised as a teacher!

Teacher: "If you breathe oxygen during the day, what do you breathe at night?"

Pupil: "Nitrogen!"

Why did the class joker go to hospital?

To learn some sick jokes!

In school assembly the piano teacher's performance was cheered and cheered.

The piano was locked up!

Teacher: "Have you thought about what you're giving your Mum for Christmas?"
Pupil: "Yes, a list of what I want!"

Where do ghosts study?

Ghoul-lege!

Teacher: "Why have you got a sausage behind your ear?"
Pupil: "Oh, no! I must have eaten my pencil for lunch!"

Why was the cannibal so popular at school?

He kept buttering up the teachers!

39

Teacher: "You missed school yesterday didn't you?"
Pupil: "Not very much!"

What happened to the carpentry teacher's car?
Wooden start!

Why are there whales at the bottom of the ocean?
Because they dropped out of school!

What after-school club do vampire children join?
A blood group!

What's the difference between teachers and chocolate?
Children like chocolate!

What's black and white and hard all over?

An exam paper!

What meals do math teachers like most?

Take aways!

Teacher: "Are you homesick?"

Pupil: "No, I'm here sick!"

Why are peacocks so unpopular in school?

They're always spreading tales!

What has a spine, but no bones?

A book!

Teacher: "What happened when electricity was discovered?"

Pupil: "Someone got a nasty shock!"

What do young ghosts write their homework in?

An exorcise book!

Teacher: "You look pale today."

Pupil: "I think I over-washed!"

Teacher: "What's the difference between ignorance and apathy?"

Pupil: "I don't know and I don't care!"

42

Tom: "Our history teacher has long black hair all the way down her back."

Josh: "It's a pity it doesn't grow on her head!"

Why did the flea fail his exams?

He wasn't up to scratch!

What's green and dangerous and good at arithmetic?

A crocodile with a calculator!

Teacher: "Are you good at arithmetic?"

Pupil: "Yes and no."

Teacher: "What do you mean?"

Pupil: "Yes, I am no good at arithmetic!"

43

Why were the school books so depressed?

They were full of problems!

What did the skunk enjoy most about school?

Show and smell!

Pupil: "Miss, can I have another glass of water?"

Cookery teacher: "But that's your tenth glass, what are you making that needs 10 glasses of water?"

Pupil: "Nothing, it's just that the notice board is still on fire!"

What's the yuckiest, stickiest, gunkiest instrument in the school orchestra?

The flu-te!

Why was Matt locked in a cage in the corner of the classroom?

He was the teacher's pet!

Where's the best place for the school sickroom?

Next to the dining hall!

What's stringy, green, wears glasses and carries a pile of books?

A bogey disguised as a teacher!

When I was at school I was as bright as the next boy...

... it's just a shame the next boy was such an idiot!

Teacher: "Why are you standing on your head?"
Pupil: "You told us to turn things over in our heads!"

What's the first thing vampires learn at school?
The alpha-bat!

Why did the nose not want to go to school?
He was always getting picked on!

Knock, knock.
Who's there?
Ida.
Ida who?
Ida awful time at school today!

Teacher: "This is the third time I've had to tell you off this week, what have you got to say about that?"

Pupil: "Thank goodness it's Friday!"

What's a mushroom?

The school dining hall!

What do you call a person who talks when nobody is listening?

A teacher!

What kind of cake do you get after school dinners?

Stomach-cake!

47

Cross-eyed Monster: "When I grow up I want to be a bus driver."

Careers Advisor: "Well I won't stand in your way!"

Teacher: "Name three collective nouns."

Pupil: "Wastepaper bin, garbage truck and vacuum cleaner!"

Teacher: "Why didn't you look up rhinos on your laptop?"

Pupil: "I didn't want a squashed lap, sir!"

Sarah: "How come you did so badly in the history test? You had all the answers written on your sleeve."

Hannah: "I had my geography shirt on by mistake!"

What's big, smelly, wears glasses and carries a pile of books?

A teacher!

What's the difference between a school teacher and a train?

One says, "Spit that gum out!" and the other says, "Choo, choo!"

Why did the one-eyed monster give up teaching?

He only had one pupil!

Teacher: "How many books have you read in your lifetime?"
Pupil: "I don't know, I'm not dead yet!"

What's the most popular sentence at school?

I don't know!

Teacher: "Why do you always get so dirty?"

Pupil: "Because I'm a lot closer to the ground than you are!"

Teacher: "Why shouldn't you mention the number 288 in polite company?"

Pupil: "Because it's two gross!"

Did you hear about the cross-eyed teacher?

He couldn't control his pupils!

What do you get if you cross the school bell with an alarm clock?

Something that wakes you up when it's time to go home!

Teacher: "If I lay one egg here and another two over there, how many eggs will there be?"

Pupil: "None."

Teacher: "Why not?"

Pupil: "Because you can't lay eggs!"

How do you keep flies out of the school dining hall?

Let them taste the food!

Teacher: "What do you call an old volcano?"

Pupil: "A blast from the past!"

Teacher: "Your work is inconsistent. Your last essay was great, but this one I can't read."

Pupil: "My Mum is a better writer than my Dad!"

51

Why did the teacher put the lights on?

Because the class was so dim!

Which school did the cannibal go to?

Eat-on!

What did Shakespeare enjoy most about school?

Play time!

The class went on a school trip to the natural history museum.

Mum: "How was it?"

Tom: "Rubbish."

Mum: "Why?"

Tom: "It's the worst zoo I've ever been to, all the animals were dead!"

What's the worst thing you will find in a school dining hall?

The food!

Teacher: "If there were five crows in a tree and the farmer shot one, how many would be left?"

Pupil: "None, they'd have all flown away!"

What's the difference between homework and onions?

Nobody cries when you chop up homework!

Teacher: "Why are you late again?"

Pupil: "There was a sign outside, it said, 'school ahead, go slow'!"

Teacher: "You can't bring that sheep into school, what about the smell?"

Pupil: "It's OK, it will soon get used to it!"

What has a Q, loads of Ps and smells bad?

School dinners!

What do you call a school jacket on fire?

A blazer!

Luke: "I think my teacher must be in love with me."

Dad: "Why?"

Luke: "Look at all the kisses she puts on my homework!"

Why did the music teacher take a ladder to school?

To help her pupils reach the high notes!

What do pixies learn at school?

The elf-abet!

Teacher: "Josh! Are you copying Tom's sums?"

Josh: "No, I'm just checking he's copied mine right!"

Knock, knock.

Who's there?

Canoe.

Canoe who?

Canoe help me with my homework?

55

Why shouldn't you put gel on your hair the day before an exam?

Because the answers might slip your mind!

Why don't ghouls get up before sunrise?

Because it never dawns on them!

Teacher: "If I say I have one hundred eyes, four wings and six legs, what would I be?"

Pupil: "A liar!"

Pupil: "Can you blame someone for something they haven't done?"

Teacher: "Of course not."

Pupil: "In that case, I haven't done my homework!"

Why did the dead boy stay home from school?

He was feeling rotten!

Teacher: "You aren't paying attention to me. Are you having trouble hearing?"

Pupil: "No, I'm having trouble listening!"

Which bird do you eat with every meal?

A swallow!

Teacher: "Well done, that's an excellent essay for someone your age."

Pupil: "What about someone my Dad's age, Miss?"

Why is the music teacher holding a shoe to his ear?

Because today's lesson is about soul music!

What did one maths book say to the other?

"I've got problems!"

What's the difference between a nice teacher and the Loch Ness Monster?

There's a chance the Loch Ness Monster might exist!

Teacher: "You've been fighting again, you've lost your two front teeth."

Pupil: "No I haven't, they're in my pocket!"

Why did the monster eat his homework?

The teacher said it was a piece of cake!

Sarah: "My teacher is like a peach?"

Molly: "You mean she's sweet?"

Sarah: "No, I mean she has a heart of stone!"

What do ghosts play in the school band?

Haunting melodies.

How do they play them?

They study the sheet music!

What kind of animals do you have to watch out for in exams?

The cheetahs!

Teacher: "Why are you crying?"

Pupil: "Sarah broke my ruler."

Teacher: "How did she do that?"

Pupil: "I hit her with it!"

59

Why did the ant come top of the class in maths?

Because he was an account-ant!

What do you get if you cross a vampire with a teacher?

Blood tests!

Teacher: "What did your parents say about your report?"

Pupil: "Do you want me to leave out the bad language?"

Teacher: "Yes."

Pupil: "Well in that case, they didn't say anything!"

How did the dinosaur do in his exam?

He passed with extinction!

Why was the turkey expelled from school?

For being fowl!

Teacher: "This homework is in your dad's handwriting."

Pupil: "Well, I did use his pen!"

What's the difference between a boring book and a boring teacher?

You can shut the book up!

Mum: "Did you get a good place in your history test?"
Josh: "Yes, I sat next to the cleverest kid in class!"

Why did the teacher jump into the lake?
Because she wanted to test the water!

What's yellow, has wheels and lies on its back?
A dead school bus!

Why shouldn't you bring your pet piranha to class?
Because they attack in schools!

Why was Luke called Space Cadet at school?
There was so much space between his ears!

What subject did the snake get an A in?
Hiss-story!

Teacher: "Where do you find the Andes?"
Pupil: "At the end of your wristies!"

Teacher: "Who broke this window?"
Pupil: "It was Molly's fault – I threw my shoe at her head and she moved!"

63

Teacher: "Why weren't you at school yesterday?"

Pupil: "I had a bad tooth."

Teacher: "Oh dear, is it better now?"

Pupil: "I'm not sure, I left it at the dentist!"

Knock, knock.

Who's there?

Harmony.

Harmony who?

Harmony times must I tell you to listen?

What did the inflatable head teacher say to the inflatable boy who brought a pin in to his inflatable school?

"You've let me down, you've let the school down and more importantly, you've let yourself down!"

What's round, red, wears glasses and carries a pile of books?

A tomato disguised as a teacher!

What do you get if you cross old potatoes with stinky mince?

School dinners!

Why did the headmaster move the chickens out of the playground?

So the pupils wouldn't overhear fowl language!

What did Shakespeare use to write with?

A pencil - either a 2B or not 2B!

Why was the chicken expelled from school?

She was always playing practical yolks!

Teacher: "I'd like to go through one whole day without having to tell you off."

Tom: "You have my permission!"

Teacher: "I asked for an essay about milk and you've only written two lines, why?"

Pupil: "I was writing about condensed milk!"

Why are witches good at English?

They're great at spelling!

Why did the teacher wear dark glasses?

Because her class was so bright!

66

What do showers and schools have in common?

One wrong turn and you're in hot water!

Mother: "Why were you sent home from school early?"

Sarah: "I set fire to something in cookery class."

Mother: "What was it?"

Sarah: "The school!"

Teacher: "Name me a deadly poison."

Pupil: "Tightrope walking."

Teacher: "That's not a poison."

Pupil: "Well, one drop and you've had it!"

What do teachers and cows have in common?

They're both moooody!

67

Scary

Who is the best dancer at the monster's ball?

The Boogie Man!

Why was the ghost hunter so fit?

He exorcised regularly!

What did the daddy cannibal say to his son at tea time?

"Don't talk with someone in your mouth!"

What do witches play at parties?

Hide-and-Shriek!

Why aren't ghosts any good at lying?

You can see right through them!

What pet does Dracula have?

A Blood Hound!

What do you call a monster that eats his mother and father?

An orphan!

What happened when the Abominable Snowman had chilli for dinner?

He melted!

What game do monsters love to play at parties?

Swallow the leader!

Why don't skeletons like roller coasters?

They don't have the guts!

Why did the zombie stay in his coffin all day?

He felt rotten!

How does a monster greet you?

Pleased to eat you!

What do you say to a three-headed monster?

"Hello, hello, hello!"

How can you help a hungry cannibal?

Give him a helping hand!

What do ghosts like on their chops?

Grave-y!

How do you make a witch itch?

Take away the W!

What does a skeleton order at a restaurant?

Spare ribs!

Why is Dracula so thin?

He eats necks to nothing!

What do sea monsters snack on between meals?

Potato ships!

Which ghost ate the three bears' porridge?

Ghoul-dilocks!

Why are zombies always tired?

Because they are dead on their feet!

What do you call a monster with a high IQ?

Frank-Einstein!

What do you call a monster who eats his father's sister?

An aunt-eater!

What music do zombies shake their stuff to?

Soul music!

What do witches use for racing each other?

Vrooom-sticks!

What fruit does Dracula like best?

Neck-tarines!

What do Italian ghosts eat?

Spook-ghetti!

Why don't cannibals eat weather forecasters?

They give them wind!

Why did the Cyclops give up teaching?

He only had one pupil!

What do sea monsters like to eat?

Fish and ships!

Why did the skeleton have no get up and go?

He was a lazy bones!

What did the father ghost say to his son?

"Spook when you're spooken to!"

What do you call a witch without a broomstick?

A witch-hiker!

What do you get when King Kong steps on Batman and Robin?

Flatman and Ribbon!

What do you get if you cross a werewolf with a cow?

A burger that bites back!

Who is the world-famous skeleton detective?

Sherlock Bones!

What does Dr. Jekyll play with his friends?

Hyde-and-seek!

What do ghosts with a sweet tooth enjoy?

Boo-ble gum!

What ride do ghosts like at the fair?

The roller-ghoster!

Two monsters are eating a clown...

... one says to the other,
"Does this taste funny to you?"

What hairstyle did the hippy monster have?

Deadlocks!

What do you call a ghost's mum and dad?

Trans-parents!

What happens when a vampire drinks too much blood?

He gets a fang-over!

How do witches keep their elaborate hairstyles in place?

Scare-spray!

What function does a witch find useful on a computer?

The spell-checker!

Who works in monster offices?

A skeleton staff!

79

Why didn't the skeleton go to the party?

He had nobody to go with!

What did the short-sighted monster wear?

Spook-tacles!

Why did the angry witch fall off her broom?

She flew off the handle!

What do posh skeletons use at dinner parties?

Bone china!

What is the correct way to greet a ghost?

"How do you boo?"

What music do mummies like to dance to?

Ragtime!

Why are zombies never lonely?

They can always dig up a few old friends!

Why are cemeteries so popular?

Who knows, but people are dying to get into them!

What kind of cheese do monsters like?

Monster-ella!

What boats do vampires sail in?

Blood vessels!

Why was the Egyptian mummy such a loner?

He was too wrapped up in himself!

Where do ghosts go on holiday?

Death Valley!

Why does Dracula enjoy ballroom dancing so much?

He loves the vaultz!

How can you tell if a zombie has a cold?

He starts coffin!

Why was the skeleton laughing?

Someone had tickled his funny bone!

What do you call
a floating sea
monster?

Bob!

What do you call
two witches that
share a room?

Broom-mates!

What did the barman say
when the ghost ordered
a gin and tonic?

"Sorry, we don't serve spirits!"

Why did the skeleton
refuse dinner?

He didn't have the
stomach for it!

What did one
cool ghost say
to the other?

"Get a life!"

What do you call a monster who hangs from the walls?

Art!

What do ghosts watch at the theatre?

Phanto-mimes!

Why is it bad news when you upset a cannibal?

You end up in hot water!

What airlines do monsters use?

British Scareways!

What do you do when you see a monster sitting in your car?

Walk!

What kind of ghosts haunt hospitals?

Surgical spirits!

What do you call a witch in the distance?

Dot!

What do you get when you cross a witch with Jack Frost?

A cold spell!

Why are vampires so artistic?

They are great at drawing blood!

What do witches sit on?

Toadstools!

Where do zombies go on holiday?

The Dead Sea!

Which dance do vampires excel in?

Fang-dango!

What do you call a skeleton rock band?

The Strolling Bones!

What is the first part of a newspaper that a monster turns to?

The horror-scope!

What do you get if you cross a snowman with a vampire?

Frostbite!

What did the monster say when he was full?

"I couldn't eat another mortal!"

What do get when you cross a vampire with a plumber?

A bloodbath!

Did you hear about the new Dracula film?

It's fang-tastic!

What do you call a monster covered in leaves?

Russell!

What do vampires do at 11am?

They take a coffin break!

What is a vampire's snack of choice?

A fang-furter!

How does a witch tell the time?

With her witch watch!

What do get if you cross a monster with a Boy Scout?

A creature that scares old ladies across the road!

What is a devil's picket line called?

A demon-stration!

Why is the graveyard so noisy?

Because of all the coffin!

What happened when Ray met a monster?

He became an ex-Ray!

What do you call
a monster with
gravy, meat and
potatoes on
his head?

Stew!

Where does
Dracula keep
his savings?

In the blood bank!

Why were the workers frightened
of their dragon boss?

He kept firing people!

When do zombies
cook their
victims?

On Fry-day!

What do you
do with a blue
monster?

Try and cheer
him up!

Who writes
invisible books?

A ghost writer!

Can you name
the famous witch
detective?

Warlock Holmes!

What's green and hides away
in bedrooms at parties?

The Incredible Sulk!

Where did the skeleton
buy his girlfriend's
birthday present?

The body shop!

Why is the
letter V like
a monster?

It comes after U!

What monster makes funny noises in its throat?

A gargoyle!

What is the best way to speak to a monster?

From a long distance!

What happened to the monster who ran away with the circus?

His mummy made him take it back!

What kind of horse would a headless horseman ride?

A knight-mare!

What do you call a yeti in a phone box?

Stuck!

Where do British witches go on holiday?

To the Isle of Fright!

Why does Dracula have no friends?

Because he's a pain in the neck!

What noise does a witch's breakfast make?

Snap, cackle and pop!

What do you call zombies in a belfry?

Dead ringers!

How do you stop a monster from smelling?

Cut off his nose!

Why did the two Cyclops flight?

They could never see eye to eye over anything!

What do you call a monster who likes sewing?

Fred!

What do you call a huge, ugly, slobbering, furry monster with cotton wool in his ears?

Anything you like, he can't hear you!

Where do ghosts pick up their mail?

At the ghost office!

What coffee does Dracula like best?

De-coffiin-ated!

What kind of monster has the best hearing?

The eeriest!

Monster: "Where do fleas go in winter?"
Werewolf: "Search me!"

If you want to know more about Dracula, what do you have to do?

Join his fang club!

What do you get if you cross a dinosaur with a wizard?

A Tyrannosaurus hex!

What kind of roads do ghosts haunt?

Dead Ends!

Who won the skeleton beauty contest?

No body!

Where do baby ghosts go during the day?

Day-scare centres!

What does a witch ask for when she goes to a hotel?

Broom-service!

Did you hear about the skeleton that was ambushed by a dog?

The dog ran off with two bones and the skeleton was left without a leg to stand on!

What is evil, ugly, dressed in black and goes round and round?

A witch in a revolving door!

What do you get if you cross a vampire with Al Capone?

A fang-ster!

What do you call a vampire that's always feeling peckish?

Snack-ula!

97

Why was
Dr. Frankenstein
never lonely?

He was good at
making friends!

How does a yeti
get to work?

By-icicle!

Why did the lady vampire give
her boyfriend mints?

Because he had bat breath!

Knock, knock.

Who's there?

Ivan.

Ivan who?

Ivan to suck
your blood!

What's big and
ugly and red
all over?

A monster in
a blender!

What's the difference between a biscuit and a monster?

It's difficult to dip a monster into your cup of tea!

What is big, hairy, stinky and has four wheels?

A werewolf on a skateboard!

What do you call a monster with a spade sticking out of his head?

Doug!

What do you call a furry wizard?

Hairy Potter!

99

Where do Abominable Snowmen go to dance?

To snowballs!

What did the angry monster do when he got his gas bill?

He exploded!

Why do witches wear name tags at the witch convention?

So they know which witch is which!

What do vampires have for lunch?

Fang-ers and mash!

What tops off a ghost's ice cream sundae?

Whipped scream!

What do you call a monster with a car on his head?

Jack!

What do you call a one-eyed monster who rides a bike?

Cycle-ops!

Did you hear about the skeleton that went out in the snow and hail without a coat, or hat?

He was a numb-skull!

What's scary and appears on a full moon wearing knickers on its head?

An underwear-wolf!

What did the skeleton say to the vampire?

"You suck!"

What kind of tie does a monster wear to a formal party?

A boo-tie!

What do you call a wicked old woman who lives by the sea?

A sand-witch!

What is evil and ugly on the inside and green on the outside?

A witch dressed as a cucumber!

What do you get if you cross a monster with a pig?

Large pork chops!

What is ugly, scary and purple?

A monster holding its breath!

What happened when the werewolf swallowed a clock?

It got ticks!

Why couldn't the swamp monster go to the party?

Because he was bogged down in his work!

What has a green spotted body, ten hairy legs and big eyes on stalks?

I don't know, but there is one crawling up your leg!

What is the American national day for vampires?

Fangs-giving Day!

What do monsters send home while on holiday?

Ghost-cards!

Why don't skeletons like the winter?

Because the cold goes right through them!

What do you call twin vampires?

Blood brothers!

What deadly monster can be found hunting in the sea at Christmas time?

Santa Jaws!

What's the scariest part of Australia?

The Northern Terror-tory!

What do you get if you cross a skeleton with a joke book?

Rib ticklers!

Where did the vampire bite the clown?

In his juggler vein!

What do you call a drunken ghost?

A methylated spirit!

What is the best thing to do if a zombie breaks down your front door?

Run out of the back door!

What do you get when you cross a vampire with a flea?

Worried dogs!

How can you tell if there's a monster in your fridge?

You can't shut the door!

What do you call a ghost policeman?

A chief in-spectre!

Has anyone ever seen the Abominable Snowman?

Not Yeti!

Why are skeletons always calm in exams?

Because nothing gets under their skin!

Did you hear about the magician who sawed people in half?

He practiced on his family. He's got two half brothers and two half sisters!

What happened to the man who couldn't keep up with his repayments to the exorcist?

He was repossessed!

What do you call a witch who goes to the beach, but won't go into the water?

A chicken sand-witch!

What was the vampire's idea of fast food?

High blood pressure!

What do you get if you cross a Scottish monster with a hamburger?

A Big Mac!

Why did Frankenstein's monster get indigestion?

He bolted down his food!

What happened to the vampires who wanted to make a movie?

They couldn't find a good crypt writer.

What do you get when you cross Bambi with a ghost?

Bam-boo!

Who protects the shores where ghosts live?

The ghost-guard!

Why did the bride of Frankenstein's monster get squeezed to death?
He had a crush on her!

What do you get if you cross a monster with a watchdog?
Very nervous postmen!

What do you call a werewolf with no legs?
Anything you like – he can't chase you!

How do you find monsters on the internet?
They use a lurch engine!

Why don't mummies like to rest?

They're afraid to unwind!

How do you make a werewolf stew?

Make him wait for 2 hours!

Alastair: "Why did the mummy miss the party?"

Rachel: "I don't know."

Alastair: "Because she was all wrapped up in her work!"

Why do witches wear green eyeshadow?

To match their teeth!

Where do vampires go fishing?

In the blood stream!

What do skeletons like to drink?

Milk- it's good for the bones!

Did you hear about the monster with eight arms?

He said they came in handy!

I heard Dr. Frankenstein is going to marry the invisible woman...

... I don't know what he sees in her!

Why do you have to wait so long for the ghost train?

Because they run a skeleton service!

What type of street does a ghost like best?

A dead end!

Why do skeletons play pianos?

Because they don't have any organs!

What do you call a vampire with no teeth?

Pointless!

What do you call a dream where you are being attacked by vampires?

A bite-mare!

What do you call a wizard on a broomstick?

A flying sorcerer!

What do you call serious rocks?

Grave stones!

How do skeletons call their friends?

On the tele-bone!

Which monster is the most untidy?

The Loch Mess Monster!

What's the first thing you should put into a haunted house?

Someone else!

What do zombies eat for dinner?

A three-corpse meal!

Why is a witch like a candle?

They are both wicked!

What did one sick casket say to the other?

Is that you coffin?

What does a monster clean his house with?

A victim cleaner!

How do vampires wash?

In a blood bath!

Monster 1: "I have a hunch."

Monster 2: "I thought you were a funny shape!"

How many people are buried in that cemetery?

All of them!

Which magical being leaves farts under your pillow?

The Toot-Fairy!

What do you get if you cross a vampire with a plumber?

A drain in the neck!

How did the stupid monster burn his face?

Bobbing for French fries!

What do vampires play poker for?

High stakes!

Why do demons and ghouls go together so well?

Because demons are a ghoul's best friend!

What do you call a skeleton snake?

A rattler!

What did the hangman say to his victim?

"Your neck's on my list!"

Why are dragons unhealthy?

Because they can't give up smoking!

Why did the monster eat five ships that were carrying potatoes?

Nobody can eat just one potato ship!

Did you hear about the monster who plugged his electric blanket into the toaster by mistake?

He spent the night popping in and out of bed!

Patient: "Doctor, doctor, I keep dreaming there are monsters playing chess under my bed. What should I do?"

Doctor: "Hide the chess set!"

Why don't ghosts like rain?
It dampens their spirits!

What happens when you talk to a stupid monster?
The words go in one ear and out of the other three!

Who are some of the werewolves' cousins?

The 'what-wolves' and the 'when-wolves'!

What do you get if you cross a monster with a chicken?

Free strange eggs!

Did you hear about the werewolf that swallowed a light bulb?

He threw it up and now he's de-lighted!

Why did the polite dragon keep burning his fingers?

Every time he coughed, he covered his mouth!

What do you get if you cross a barber with a ghost?

A 'scare-dresser'!

Monster 1: "Stand still, there's something hairy and ugly on your shoulder."
Monster 2: "Help, what is it?"
Monster 1: "Oh, it's just your head!"

What's a flesh-eater's most common side-dish?

Human beans!

What do you get if you cross an Italian landmark with a ghost?

The Screaming Tower of Pisa!

Why did the monster cut off the top of his head?

He wanted to keep an open mind!

Why did the vampire stay up so late?

He was studying for his blood test!

What did the mortician ask, as he was walking to the crematorium?

"What's cooking?"

What did Dr. Frankenstein do when the monster's head fell off?

He made a bolt for it!

Which monsters get the most girlfriends?

The good-lurking ones!

What should you do if you meet a skeleton in a dark alley?

Jump out of your skin and say hello!

Why did Dracula's girlfriend dump him?

The relationship was very draining!

What do you call a dead chicken that haunts you at night?

A poultry-geist!

Why did the stupid monster get so excited after he finished his jigsaw puzzle in six months?

Because it said '2-4 years' on the box!

Why couldn't the skeleton fart in a crowded lift?

It didn't have the guts!

What do you get if you cross a computer virus with a vampire?

A nasty byte!

Why did the monster knit herself three socks?

Because she grew another foot!

Why did the cannibal eat the brains of his victims?

It gave him food for thought!

Did you hear about the comedian who entertained at the werewolf's party?

He had them howling in the aisles!

Werewolf 1: "Grrrr."

Werewolf 2: "Grrrr, grrrrr, nerrrgg."

Werewolf 1: "Don't change the subject!"

What did Dracula say to his new apprentice?

"We needed some fresh blood around here!"

What do you get when you cross a vampire with a nun?

A nasty habit!

What kind of tiles did the witch have installed in her bathroom?

Rep-tiles!

What did the Big Bad Wolf say when he got a stomach ache?

"Maybe it was someone I ate!"

What is large, yellow, lives in Scotland and has never been seen?

The Loch Ness Canary!

What do you call a bunch of man-eaters that like sweaty feet?

Odor-eaters!

What happened when King Kong swallowed Big Ben?

He found it time consuming!

What do you call a skeleton that won't get out of bed?

Lazy bones!

Monster 1: "I'm so thirsty my tongue is hanging out."

Monster 2: "Oh, I thought that was your necktie!"

A monster and a zombie went to a funeral home.

"I'd like to order a coffin for a friend of mine who has recently died," said the monster.

"Certainly, Sir," said the undertaker, **"but you didn't have to bring him with you!"**

What's worse than being a 300-pound witch?

Being her broomstick!

How do vampires keep their breath smelling nice?

They use extractor fangs!

What happened when Frankenstein's monster swallowed plutonium?

He got atomic ache!

Sarah: "The police are looking for a monster with one eye."

Molly: "Why don't they use both their eyes?"

What do you call a skeleton who presses a doorbell?

A dead ringer!

History

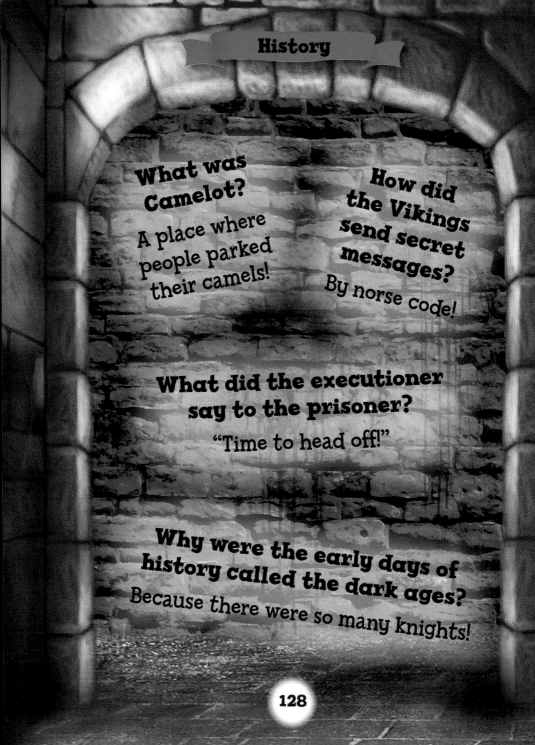

What was Camelot?

A place where people parked their camels!

How did the Vikings send secret messages?

By norse code!

What did the executioner say to the prisoner?

"Time to head off!"

Why were the early days of history called the dark ages?

Because there were so many knights!

Which king had the noisiest bottom?

King Richard the Lion-fart!

Who made King Arthur's round table?

Sir-Cumference!

Why did Henry VIII have so many wives?

He liked to chop and change!

Why is the ghost of Anne Boleyn always running after the ghost of Henry VIII?

She's trying to get ahead!

Why did Robin Hood only rob the rich?

Because the poor didn't have anything worth stealing!

What's vicious, Victorian and lives at the bottom of the sea?

Jack the Kipper!

Where did knights learn to kill dragons?

At knight school!

What do you call a Roman emperor with the flu?

Julius Sneezer!

Did you hear about the Roman slave who had his ears chopped off as punishment?

He was never heard of again!

Did you hear about the tense mummy?

He was really wound up!

What do you call a pirate with four eyes?

A piiiirate!

Why was the Egyptian prince so upset?

He woke up to find his Daddy was now a Mummy!

Why did the one-handed pirate cross the road?

He wanted to get to the second-hand shop!

Where does Napoleon keep his armies?

Up his sleevies!

How was the Roman Empire cut in half?

With a pair of rusty Caesars!

Why did the knight pull out of the archery contest?

He found it an arrowing experience!

What did the dragon say when he saw the knight in shining armor?

"I hate tinned food!"

What did Caesar say after Brutus stabbed him?

"Ow!"

Why do mummies not tell secrets?

They keep everything under wraps!

Did you hear about the time Henry VIII farted in court?

It caused a royal stink!

What was the fruit that launched a thousand ships?

Melon of Troy!

Which queen burped a lot?

Queen Hictoria!

Why was King Arthur's army too tired to fight?

Too many sleepless knights!

What do you put on the gravestone of a knight in shining armor?

Rust in peace!

What happened when Queen Victoria farted?

She issued a royal pardon!

Why did the executioner start work early?

He wanted to get a-head!

Where were traitors beheaded?

Just above their shoulders!

Why did Anne Boleyn not stand still when she was being executed?

She fancied a run around the block!

What's a gelatine?

An ancient device for chopping the heads off jelly babies!

What do kings do with their rotting teeth?

Get them crowned!

Who was England's smelliest king?

Richard the Turd!

What did the executioner say to the criminal in the guillotine?

"Heads, I win!"

Queen Victoria was on the throne from 1837 to 1901...

... that's a bad case of constipation!

When did Henry VIII die?

Just before they buried him!

Who was the most reasonable king of Egypt?

Pharaoh Nuff!

Why did Julius Ceasar buy permanent ink pens?

He wanted to 'Mark Anthony' forever!

Why did Cleopatra take milk baths?

She couldn't find a cow tall enough for a shower!

What's brown and sits on a piano stool?

Mozart's last movement!

Where do executioners work?

Head office!

Why is it always so yucky and wet in Britain?

The kings and queens keep reigning!

What do you call a mosquito in chain mail?

A bite in shining armor!

What kind of lighting did Noah use for the ark?

Flood lights!

What did William the Conqueror say when he fell down the loo?

"Weeeeeeeeeeeeee!"

What happened when the gladiator put his head in the lion's mouth to count his teeth?

The lion closed his mouth to see how many heads the gladiator had!

What game did
King Arthur like
playing most?

Knights and crosses!

What's a
guillotine?

A pain in
the neck!

What's two hundred years
old and lies at the bottom
of the ocean, twitching?

A nervous wreck!

What did the prisoner say
when he was put on the rack?

"Looks as if I'll be here for
a l-o-n-g stretch!"

Which Egyptian queen liked to walk around in her underwear?

Cleo-pantra!

What do executioners write in December?

Their Christmas chopping lists!

During which age did the mummies live?

The band-age!

What do you call a highwayman with a cough and a dribble of snot running from his nose?

Sick Turpin!

What do Alexander the Great and Kermit the Frog have in common?

The same middle name!

What did dinosaurs have that no others animals ever had?

Baby dinosaurs!

What do pirates use soap for?

To wash themselves ashore!

What did the WWI cannon say to the WWII mine?

"You're a blast!"

Why would you use Cleopatra to draw a straight line?

She was an ancient ruler!

How much did the captain's treasure cost?

An arm and a leg!

What's purple and burns?

The Grape Fire of London!

Which historical figure was an expert on the springboard?

Lady Good-diver!

Why did it take Long John Silver so long to learn the alphabet?

He spent years at 'C'!

What was the middle ages famous for?

Its knight life!

What do you get in a five star pyramid?

A tomb with a view!

Who succeeded the first President of the United States?

The second one!

What would you get hanging from the walls of a Tudor castle?

Tired arms!

What is Queen Vic short for?

So she can tickle her toes!

What did the pirate say as he fell over board?

Water-way to go!

What do you call a Tyrannosaurus rex that talks and talks and talks?

A dino-bore!

What do hangmen read?

Noose-papers!

What is Beethoven doing in his grave?

De-composing!

Where did the Vikings land when they invaded Britain?

On their feet!

Why was the pirate cross when the toilet was out of order?

Because any pirate without a 'p' becomes irate!

Where do pirates go to let their hair down?

The beach ball!

Why are there old dinosaur bones in the museum?

Because they can't afford new ones!

Why is history like an old fruit cake?

It's full of dates!

What do you call a sleeping dinosaur?

A dino-snore!

What's the difference between a pirate and a bargain hunter?

One sails the sea, the other sees the sales!

Why do dinosaurs eat raw meat?

Because they don't know how to cook!

What do you call a caveman who's been buried since the stone age?

Pete!

How do you use an ancient Egyptian doorbell?

Toot-and-come-in!

When did the Vikings invade Britain?

During a plunder storm!

Why did King Arthur have a round table?

So no one could corner him!

Why do cavemen avoid dinosaurs?

Because their eggs stink!

Did you hear the dirty rumour about the empty pyramid?

There was nothing in it!

What do you call a pirate who lives at the bottom of the sea?

Billy the Squid!

Why did the dinosaur cross the road?

The chicken hadn't been invented yet!

What does a Triceratops sit on?

Its Tricera-bottom!

Why were the Duke of York's men so tired on April 1st?

They had just completed a 31 day March!

Why did the dinosaurs become extinct?

Because they wouldn't take a bath!

How do mummies hide?

They use masking tape!

Who designed Noah's ark?

An ark-itect!

What was the greatest accomplishment of the early Romans?

Speaking Latin!

What do you call a Tyrannosaurus rex when it wears a cowboy hat and boots?

Tyrannosaurus Tex!

How do you make a Victoria Cross?

Stamp on her toes!

Why do dragons sleep during the day?

So they can fight knights!

How do we know that Roman builders worked best in the dark?

Because Rome wasn't built in a day!

Why did Captain Cook sail to Australia?

It was too far to swim!

What makes more noise than a dinosaur?

Two dinosaurs!

What did the boy mummy say to the girl mummy?

"Em-balmy about you!"

Why did the mammoth have a fur coat?

He would have looked silly in a blazer!

Creepy Crawlies

Creepy Crawlies

What do you call an ant in space?

An ant-ronaut!

What is brown one minute and white the next minute?

A worm in a freezer!

Why was the bug hit with an on-the-spot fine?

It was a litterbug!

What do you call a musical insect?

A humbug!

How do you start an insect race?

One, two, flea, go!

What music do insects listen to?

The Beetles!

What insect runs away from the scene of a crime?

A flea!

What's black, has eight legs and a trunk?

A spider going on holiday!

Which Roman emperor was actually a mouse?

Julius Cheeser!

Creepy Crawlies

What's grey and hairy and lives on a man's top lip?

A mouse-tash!

How can you tell if a spider is angry?

It goes up the wall!

What creepy crawlies do cats like to lean against?

Caterpillars!

What is the largest ant?

An eleph-ant!

Where do bees go on vacation?

The wax museum!

What do you give a snake with a headache?

Asp-rin!

Why do bees buzz?

They find it difficult to whistle!

Who do wasps like to listen to?

Sting!

What bee is hard to hear?

A mumble bee!

What did the wasp say to the bee?

"Your honey or your life!"

Creepy Crawlies

What do you get if you cross ants with a rabbit?

Bugs Bunny!

Why were the little beetles grounded?

They were bugging their parents!

What was the worm doing in the corn field?

Going in one ear and out the other!

What do you call a bug that's worked its way to the top?

Head lice!

**What do you call
tired bugs?**

Sleepy crawlies!

What do you call a fly with no wings?

A walk!

**What do you call a fly with
no wings or legs?**

A raisin!

**What do you get if you cross an
electric eel with a sponge?**

A shock absorber!

What's wriggly, dangerous and goes, "Hith, hith"?

A snake with a lisp!

Where do ill wasps go?

Wasp-ital!

Where do wasps and bees go for their holidays?

Sting-apore!

What did the bee say to the flower?

"Hello honey!"

Why are moths so unpopular?

They pick holes in everything!

What type of bee is good for your health?

Vitamin B-ee!

What do bees chew?

Bumble gum!

Why did the hedgehog cross the road?

To see his squash partner!

"Waiter, there are two flies in my soup!"

"Don't worry, Sir, we don't charge for the extra one!"

What do you call fishing when you don't catch any fish?

Drowning worms!

What lives in gum trees?

Stick insects!

Why did the lizard go on a diet?

It weighed too much for its scales!

Why did the blob always stay home?

He had no place to goo!

Why did the moth nibble a hole in the carpet?

He wanted to see the floor show!

What did the bus driver say to the Frog?

"Hop on!"

Why did the mosquito go to the dentist?

To improve his bite!

How many legs does an ant have?

The same as your uncle!

What did the slime say to the mould when they saw each other after a long time?

"You gruesome since I saw you last!"

Creepy Crawlies

How do you know when a mouse needs oiling?

It squeaks!

What has antlers and sucks blood?

A moose-quito!

What is the difference between a fly and a bird?

A bird can fly, but a fly can't bird!

What is the most faithful insect?

A flea, once they find someone they stick to them!

What game do elephants play with ants?

Squash!

What do you call two spiders who just got married?

Newly-webs!

What kind of bees fight?

Rumble bees!

What has six legs, bites and talks in code?

A morse-quito!

What did the fly say when he hit the car windscreen?

"That's me all over!"

Why was the insect thrown out of the forest?

Because he was a litter bug!

Patient: "Doctor, doctor, I keep thinking I'm a caterpillar."

Doctor: "Don't worry, you'll change soon!"

What's the difference between a worm and a cockroach?

Cockroaches crunch more when you eat them!

"Waiter, there's a dead beetle in my gravy."

"Yes, Sir. Beetles are terrible swimmers!"

What did the spider say to the beetle?

"Stop bugging me!"

Where do you find giant snails?

At the end of a giant's finger!

Patient: "Doctor, doctor, I keep seeing insects flying around my head."

Doctor: "It's just a bug that's going around!"

What do you get if you cross a baby and a spider?

A creepy crawler!

Which creepy crawlies are at the cutting edge of technology?

Spiders, they have their own websites!

What's the scariest insect?

A zom-bee!

What did the snake say when he was offered a piece of cheese for dinner?

"Thank you, I'll just have a slither!"

What did one slug say to another who had hit him and rushed off?

"I'll get you next slime!"

What did the slug say as he slipped down the window very fast?

"How slime flies!"

How do you know your kitchen is filthy?

The slugs leave trails on the floor that read, 'clean me'!

What do you get if you cross a glow-worm with a pint of beer?

Light ale!

171

What did the woodworm say to the chair?

"It's been nice gnawing you!"

What did one maggot say to another?

"What's a nice girl like you doing in a joint like this?"

What is the best advice to give a worm?

Sleep late!

What kind of wig can hear?

An earwig!

How do you keep flies out of the kitchen?

Put a pile of manure in the living room!

172

Why did the fly fly?

Because the spider spied 'er!

What do you get if you cross a computer with a million mosquitos?

A gigabyte!

What goes 'snap, crackle and pop'?

A firefly with a short circuit!

What did the spider say when he broke his new web?

"Darn it!"

What did the two spiders say to the fly?

"We're getting married do you want to come to the webbing?"

How do snails get their shells so shiny?

They use snail varnish!

What did the maggot say to his friend when he got stuck in an apple?

"Worm your way out of that one!"

What is life like for a wood worm?

Boring!

Why didn't the two worms get on Noah's Ark in an apple?

Because everyone had to go on in pairs!

What do you get if you cross a rabbit and fleas?

Bugs Bunny!

What is the difference between a flea-bitten dog and a bored visitor?

Ones going to itch and the other is itching to go!

What did one flea say to the other after a night out?

"Shall we walk home or take a dog?"

Two spiders were running across the top of a cereal box. One says to the other, "Why are we running so fast?"

"Because it says tear along the dotted line!"

What do you call a stupid flea?

A looney-tic!

What do you call a nervous insect?

A jitterbug!

What is the definition of a caterpillar?

A worm in a fur coat!

What do you get if you cross a centipede and a chicken?

Enough drumsticks to feed an army!

Why was the centipede dropped from the insect football team?

He took too long to put his boots on!

What is green and can jump a mile in a minute?

A grasshopper with hiccups!

Why wouldn't they let the butterfly into the dance?

Because it was a moth ball!

Where would you put an injured insect?

In an ant-bulance!

Creepy Crawlies

What do insects learn at school?

Moth-matics!

What do bats sing when it rains?

"Raindrops keep falling on my feet!"

What's the biggest moth in the world?

A mam-moth!

Knock, knock.

Who's there?

Amos.

Amos who?

A mosquito bit me!

What sits in the middle of the world wide web?

A very, very big spider!

How do fleas travel around?

Itch-hiking!

What opera do snakes love to go to?

Wrigg-o-letto!

What has 50 feet but can't walk?

Half a centipede!

What happens when you put a glowworm in water?

It becomes a floodlight!

What lies on the ground, one hundred feet up in the air?

A dead centipede!

Which insect tells the time?

A clock-roach!

What flies, has stripes and is very clumsy?

A fumble bee!

Did you hear about the two silkworms who had a race?

It ended in a tie!

What's green and dangerous?

A frog stampede!

What do you get if you cross a bag of snakes with a cupboard full of food?

Snakes and larders!

Why did the toad sit on the mushroom?

He thought it was a toad-stool!

What's the last thing to go through a fly's mind as it crashes into the windshield?

Its rear end!

Why did the termite eat a sofa and two chairs?

It had a suite tooth!

What do you call a man who catches blue bottles with a fishing rod?

A fly fisherman!

How does the bee get to school?

It takes the school buzz!

What kind of bugs live on the moon?

Lunar ticks!

Did you hear about the pregnant bedbug?

She had her baby in the spring!

Which sport is a mosquito best at?

Skin diving!

What did the spider do when she couldn't carry the stick on her own?

She hired an assist-ant!

What's the best way to prevent getting sick from biting insects?

Stop biting them!

What do frogs eat for breakfast?

Croako-pops!

What's the difference between head lice and dandruff?

Lice crunches more when you eat it!

What did the banana say to the maggot?

You're boring me to death!

What's the difference between an earthworm and a cookie?

An earthworm doesn't fall apart when you dunk it in milk!

If I have eight flies on my desk and swat one, how many are left?

Just one - the dead one!

What did the bug say when it hit the windshield?

"I don't have the guts to do that again!"

Knock, knock.

Who's there?

Harry.

Harry who?

Harry, scary spider crawling on you!

Craig: "I once ate a slimy slug in my pyjamas."

Ethan: "Really?"

Craig: "Yes, I still don't know howhe got into them!"

What did the cowboy maggot say when he walked into a saloon?

"Give me a slug of whiskey!"

If ants are so busy, how come they find time to turn up at picnic?

What do you do with a scorpion the size of a horse?

Ride it to hospital after it stings you!

What do you get if you cross a centipede with a homing pigeon?

A creepy crawler that just keeps coming back!

Sports

Who came last in the Winter Olympics?

The Abominable Slowman!

How do vampire footballers wash?

They all get in the bat tub!

Patient: "Doctor, doctor, I feel like a tennis racquet."

Doctor: "Yes, you do seem highly strung!"

What happened when two huge monsters ran in a race?

One ran in short bursts, the other one ran in burst shorts!

How do ghosts keep fit?

With regular exorcise!

What do you call a non-swimmer who falls in a river?

Bob!

What's sport do vampire's like best?

Bat-minton!

Why did the monster sit on a pumpkin?

It wanted to play squash!

What do you do if you split your sides laughing?

Run until you get a stitch in them!

Why did the ballerina quit?

Because it was tu-tu hard!

Who is the most important member of the ghost's football team?

The ghoulie!

Why did the surfer stop surfing?

Because the sea weed!

Who won the world's strongest vegetable contest?

The muscle sprout!

What do you get if you cross an England footballer with a chicken?

David Peckham!

Who won the vampires' race?

It was neck and neck!

What's the hardest part about skydiving?

The ground!

Why are babies good at basketball?

Because they're great dribblers!

What goes in pink and comes out blue?

A swimmer on a cold day!

Matt: "The teacher said I would be on the football team except for two things."

Dad: "What are they?"

Matt: "My feet!"

Why do basketball players carry hankies around with them?

They are always dribbling!

How did the football pitch turn into a triangle?

Someone took a corner!

If you have a referee in football and an umpire in tennis, what do you have in bowls?

A goldfish!

Which athlete is always warm?

The long jumper!

Why did the midfielder refuse to travel by plane?

He didn't want to be put on the wing!

How do footballers stay cool during the game?

They stand close to the fans!

Why did the monster take two pairs of socks to the golf course?

In case he got a hole-in-one!

What do you get if you cross a martial artist with a pig?

A pork chop!

What do boxers like to drink?

Fruit punch!

What animal is best at hitting a baseball?

A bat!

Did you hear about the crazy monster who wanted to listen to the match?

He burnt his ear!

What lights up a football stadium?

A football match!

Why was the turkey sent off in the football game?

Fowl play!

Did you hear about the ghosts' race?

It was a dead heat!

What do magicians and footballers have in common?

They both do hat tricks!

Why is tennis so noisy?

Every player raises a racquet!

What has five heads, ten legs and is purple?

A basketball team holding their breath!

Did you hear about the monster who exploded during the race?

He bust a gut trying to win!

Tom: "How are you getting on with your trampoline lessons?"
Josh: "Oh, you know, up and down!"

What do monsters play when they are in their mum's car?

Squash!

What do cheerleaders eat for breakfast?

Cheerios!

Which weight do ghosts box at?

Phantom weight!

Why are running shoes like spotty boys?

They both have pimples on their bottoms!

Why should bowling alleys be quiet?

So you can hear a pin drop!

What do vampire footballers eat at halftime?

Blood oranges!

A mountaineer got into difficulties when he was dangling from a rope over the edge of a precipice. As his friend began to pull him up, the rope started to fray.

"What will we do if the rope breaks?" asked the man, fearfully.

"Don't worry," called the other man. **"I've got another!"**

What's the difference between a nail and a boxer?

One gets knocked in, the other gets knocked out!

What did the monster say when he accidentally burped during the match?

"Sorry, it was a freak-hic!"

Why did Richard's rugby team always win?

Their feet smelt so bad that the other teams would never dare tackle them!

Why are fairy godmothers surprisingly good football coaches?

They always help you get to the ball!

What do ghosts say when a girl footballer is sent off?

"Ban-she, ban-she!"

Why can't you tell a joke whilst ice skating?

The ice might crack up!

Why did the basketball player go to the doctor?

To get more shots!

Which animal can jump higher than a house?

All of them.
Houses can't jump!

What happened when the martial artist joined the army?

He saluted and knocked himself out!

Why was Cinderella kicked off the football team?

She kept running away
from the ball!

Where do fruits play cricket?

On the cricket peach!

Why do footballers make bad dinner dates?

They dribble too much!

Why was Cinderella rubbish at tennis?

Her coach was a pumpkin!

What is the naughtiest sport?

Bad-minton!

Which international cricket team plays half dressed?

The 'Vest' Indies!

How can you swim 100 meters in a few seconds?

Go over a waterfall!

Why was the monster baseball team arrested?

There were reports of a hit and run!

Why was the computer so good at golf?

Because it had a hard drive!

Tom: "You've got your boots on the wrong feet."

Josh: "They're the only feet I've got!"

Why should you never hold a sports day in the jungle?

There are too many cheetahs!

Why didn't the dog want to play football?

It was a boxer!

How long does it take to learn to ice skate?

A few sittings!

Did you hear about the stinky footballer?

He was scent off!

Why do basketball players love donuts?

Because they dunk them!

203

Manager: "Richard, why have you brought a broom to football practice?"

Richard: "You said I was going to play sweeper!"

What time of year is it best to jump on a trampoline?

Spring!

What game do wizard octopuses play?

Squid-ditch!

What song do cross-channel swimmers always sing?

"Please re-grease me!"

What do monster runners do when they forget something?

They jog their memory!

Why was the ball dribbling?

You'd dribble too if your head was bouncing off the floor!

Did you hear about the tap dancer?

He fell into the sink!

What runs around a football pitch but doesn't move?

A fence!

What did the monster find harder to catch, the faster he ran?

His breath!

Who won the world's strongest fruit contest?

The sat-sumo wrestler!

Why is it boring watching an alien football match in space?

There is no atmosphere!

Why do elephants have grey trunks?
They are all on the same swimming team!

What does baseball have in common with pancakes?

The both rely on the batter!

What do you call a bike that keeps biting people?

A vicious cycle!

Why are shoes like a losing basketball team?

They hate to suffer defeat!

Which creepy crawly is not a good choice for goal keeper?

'Fumble' bee!

Why didn't the nose make the body part football team?

It wasn't picked!

Why is it so hard to break into the sport of sword-fighting?

It's a cut-throat industry!

What should you do if the football pitch floods during play?

Bring on the subs!

Did you hear the joke about the jump rope?

No, I skipped it!

What do you get if you cross a lake with a leaky boat?

About halfway!

Sports

Why do some people swim backstroke?

Because you should never swim on a full stomach!

What's the best animal to take along when you go swimming?

A gi-raft!

Why did the football team made-up of artists, never win?

They liked to draw!

Why did the monster take up boxing?

He wanted to improve his looks!

How did Pinocchio win all of his races?

By a nose!

209

A marathon runner ran for three hours, but only moved two feet.
How come?

He only had two feet!

P.E. teacher: "Don't dive into that swimming pool, there's no water in it!"

Pupil: "It's OK, I can't swim!"

Tom: "My P.E. teacher wouldn't listen to me when I said I was no good at throwing the javelin."

Josh: "What happened?"

Tom: "She got the point eventually!"

How is playing the bagpipes like throwing a javelin blindfolded?

You don't have to be good to get everyone's attention!

What's the hardest part about ice-skating?

The ice!

How do you service your pogo stick?

Give it a spring clean!

What do you call a bunch of chess players bragging in a hotel lobby at Christmas?

Chess nuts boasting in an open foyer!

Animals

What's green and goes round at 100 miles an hour?

A frog in a washing machine!

What do cats have for a Friday night treat?

Special fried mice!

What's small, cuddly and bright purple?

A koala holding its breath!

What did the bear eat when he had toothache?

The dentist!

What do you give an elephant that's going to be sick?

Plenty of space!

What do you get if you cross a cow with a camel?

Lumpy milkshakes!

What do you call a bear with its ear cut off?

B!

What's yellow, sticky and smells of bananas?

Monkey sick!

Why aren't elephants allowed on beaches?

They can't keep their trunks up!

How do you find where a flea has bitten you?

Start from scratch!

What do cats put in their lemonade?

Mice cubes!

What do you get if you cross a duck with a firework?

A fire-quacker!

What do you get when you cross a cow with a grass cutter?

A lawn moo-er!

What's bright red and weighs four tons?

An elephant with a knot in its trunk!

What do you get if you cross a skunk and an owl?

A bird that smells, but doesn't give a hoot!

What's big, grey and wears a mask?

The Ele-phantom of the Opera!

What do you call a frozen cat?

A cat-cicle!

Farmer: "I had to shoot the cow."

Farmer's wife: "Was he mad?"

Farmer: "He wasn't too happy about it!"

What do camels wear on hunting trips?

Camel-flage!

Is chicken soup good for you?

Not if you're a chicken!

What is a running chicken called?

Poultry in motion!

Why are elephants wrinkly?

Because they don't fit on the ironing board!

What's pink and hard?

A flamingo wearing knuckle dusters!

What do you call a sleeping bull?

A bull-dozer!

What do you call a baby whale?

A little squirt!

What's black, white and noisy?

A zebra with a drum kit!

What do you call a frog with no back legs?

Unhoppy!

What's blue and has big ears?

An elephant at the North Pole!

How do you make a gorilla cross?

Nail two together!

What do you call a fish with no eyes?

Fsh!

What's black, white and red all over?

A zebra in a blender!

Patient: "Doctor, doctor, I keep thinking I'm a goat."

Doctor: "And how long has this been going on?"

Patient: "Oh, ever since I was a kid!"

What has webbed feet and fangs?

Count Quack-ula!

What sort of math do cows do?

Cow-culus!

How do you catch a squirrel?

Climb up a tree and act like a nut!

Tom: "My dog has no nose."

Josh: "How does it smell?"

Tom: "Awful!"

What should you do if you come across two snails fighting?

Leave them to slug it out!

What do you give a sick pig?

Oink-ment!

What do you get if you cross a hippo with an earthworm?

Giant holes in the garden!

What is a crocodile's favourite game?

Snap!

What do you call a cow with no legs?

Ground beef!

What's big and hairy and sits in the corner facing the wall?

A naughty gorilla!

Why can't Bob ride a bike?

Because Bob's a fish!

What do you call a lamb with a machine gun?

Lamb-o!

What do you call an elephant that never washes?

A smelly-phant!

Where does Superman's goldfish live?

In a superbowl!

Why is it difficult to eat chocolate moose?

The antlers get stuck in your throat!

What do you do when an elephant sneezes?

Run!

Which animal has the biggest bum?

A hippo-bottomus!

What do you do if you find a poisonous snake in your toilet?
Wait till he's finished!

What do you get if you cross a parrot with a seagull?
A bird that makes a mess on your head, then apologizes!

Tom: "Our parrot lays square eggs."
Josh: "Does it talk?"
Tom: "Yes, but it can only say one word."
Josh: "What's that?"
Tom: "Ouch!"

Animals

What do you call a gorilla with bananas in his ears?

Anything, he can't hear you!

What do you get if you cross a cow, a sheep and a goat?

The milky-baa kid!

What are crisp, like milk and go 'eek, eek, eek' when you eat them?

Mice Krispies!

What's invisible and smells of bananas?

Monkey farts!

Why did the chameleon have a nervous breakdown?

He was sat on a tartan rug!

What's big and grey and squirts green gunk at you?

An elephant with the flu!

What happens when a cat licks a lemon?

It turns into a sour puss!

What has six eyes but cannot see?

Three blind mice!

What do you call a pig with no clothes on?

Streaky bacon!

What do you get if you cross a science fiction film with a toad?

Star Warts!

How do hedgehogs play leap-frog?

Very carefully!

How can you tell when a moth farts?

It flies in a straight line for a second!

What wears a coat all summer and pants all winter?

A dog!

What's invisible and smells of nuts?

Squirrel farts!

What do you call a headless sheep with no legs?

A cloud!

What do you call a pig that does karate?

Pork chop!

Little birdie flying high, dropped a message from the sky...

... "Oh," said the farmer, wiping his eye, "it's a good job that cows can't fly!"

What do you get if you feed gunpowder to a chicken?

An egg-splosion!

What do you get if you cross a chicken with a cement mixer?

A brick layer!

Why did the farmer give his chickens whisky?

He wanted scotch eggs!

How do you con sheep?

Pull the wool over their eyes!

What do you get if you cross some nuns with a chicken?

A pecking order!

What do you call a three-legged ass?

A wonkey donkey!

How do you make ice-cream?

Put a cow in the freezer!

Which animal has a lot of gas?

An aard-fart!

What did the leopard say after he had devoured a gazelle?

"That hit the spots!"

What is out of bounds?

A tired kangaroo!

What do you call a rubbish lion tamer?

Claude B. Hinde!

What smells like eucalyptus?

Koala farts!

What sort of dog has no tail and no legs?

A hot dog!

What do you get if you cross a bird with a snake?

A feather boa!

What goes 'ha, ha, ha, plop'?

A hyena laughing its head off!

Why did the stag wear braces?

He had buck teeth!

Why did the chicken cross the road?

To prove it had guts!

What has 4 wheels and flies?

A stinky wheely bin!

What's the difference between a flea and a wolf?

One prowls on the hairy, the other howls on the prairie!

What is another word for a python?

A mega-bite!

Why did the octopus blush?

It saw the ocean's bottom!

Josh: "I keep a pig under my bed."

Tom: "What about the smell?"

Josh: "He doesn't mind!"

Why do elephants stomp on people?

They like the squishy feeling between their toes!

What do you get if you cross a jellyfish with an elephant?

Jelly the elephant!

What goes eek, eek, bang?

A mouse in a minefield!

What did the monkey do when he lost his tail?

He went to the re-tailer!

How does a bird with a broken wing land safely?

With a sparrow-chute!

Why do gorillas have big nostrils?

Because they have big fingers!

Patient: "Doctor, doctor, I keep thinking I'm a sheep."

Doctor: "Really? And how do you feel about that?"

Patient: "Very baaaaaaad!"

What's green, slimy and drips from trees?

Giraffe bogies!

Why do birds fly south for the winter?

It's too far to walk!

Where does a horse go when he gets sick?

The horse-pital!

Did you hear about the sunburnt shark?

He was basking for it!

"Doctor doctor, I feel like a frog. I'm afraid I could croak at any moment!"

What type of fish performs operations?

A sturgeon!

What do you call a woodpecker with no beak?

A headbanger!

235

What do you get it you cross a piranha and a nose?

I don't know, but I wouldn't pick it!

What has two grey legs and two brown legs?

A hippopotamus with diarrhea!

Jason: "I've just been thrown out of the zoo for feeding the monkeys."

Lauren: "What? Why?"

Jason: "I fed them to the lions!"

What is dry on the outside, filled with water and blows up buildings?

A fish tank!

Why was the crab not very good at sharing?

He was shell-fish!

Why are skunks always arguing?

Because they like to raise a stink!

What happens when you put a mouse in the freezer?

You get mice cubes!

Why do giraffes have such long necks?

Have you ever smelt a giraffe fart?

What kind of snake is good at maths?

An adder!

Did you hear about the dog that lay down to eat a bone?

When it stood up it only had three legs!

How many skunks does it take to make a big stink?

A phew!

What did the farmer call the cow that would not give him any milk?

An udder disgrace!

Why did the pig go to the casino?

To play the slop machines!

What do you call a girl with a frog in her hair?

Lily!

What's yellow and goes round at 100 miles an hour?

A mouldy frog in a washing machine!

What do you give a pony with a cold?

Cough-stirrup!

How did the pig get to hospital?

In a ham-bulance!

What clothes do fleas wear to work?

Jump suits!

What kind of creature is made out of wood?

A timber wolf!

What happened when the cow jumped over the barbed-wire fence?

It was an udder catastrophe!

What do you call a donkey with one eye and three legs?

A winky wonky donkey!

What happens when you cross a girl jellyfish and a boy jellyfish?

Jelly babies!

What do you get when a cow gets caught in an earthquake?

Milkshake!

What was written on the turkey's gravestone?

Roast in peace!

What do you call a cow that can go in the washing machine?

Washer-bull!

What do you get if you cross a pig with a centipede?

Bacon and legs!

What type of dog runs away from frying pans?

A sausage dog!

What was the canary doing in prison?

It was a jailbird!

What do you call a row of rabbits walking backwards?

A receding hare line!

How do you know when your cat's eaten a duck?

It looks down in the mouth!

Why do cats have fur balls?

Because they love a good gag!

What do you call
a dog with a cold?

Achoo-huahua!

What do you
give a dog with a
temperature?

Mustard – it's the
best thing for
a hot dog!

What happened when the
dog went to the flea circus?

It stole the show!

What do you call
a dog that digs
up bones?

A barky-ologist!

What do you call a
mouse with no legs?

Cat food!

Animals

Why did the lobster blush?

Because the sea weed!

When does your hamster drive your car?

When you're not looking!

Walrus: "What's your name?"

Polar Bear: "My name is...................Clive."

Walrus: "Why the long pause?"

Polar Bear: "I've always had them!"

Why did the stupid chicken climb over the glass wall?

To see what was on the other side!

What did one pig say the other?

Let's be pen pals!

How does a group of dolphins make a decision?

Flipper coin!

What happened to the octopus that deserted the army?

He had to face the firing squid!

How do you save a hippo drowning in hot chocolate?

Throw in a marshmallow!

Why do coyotes call at night?

The rates are cheaper!

What should an elephant do if it breaks a toe?

Give up ballet dancing!

Why don't rhinos eat pickled onions?

Because they can't get their heads in the jar!

What musical key do cows sing in?

Beef-flat!

What would you do if you kept two hundred goldfish in the bathtub and you wanted to take a bath?

Blindfold them!

Did you hear about the deer who took his driving test?

The examiner passed the buck!

Why do sharks live in salt water?

Because if they were in pepper water they would sneeze!

Why do mother kangaroos hate rainy days?

Because the kids have to play inside!

How do you spot a bald eagle?

All its feathers are combed over to one side!

Did you hear about the stupid wolf?

It got stuck in a trap, chewed off three legs and was still stuck!

Why don't elephants smoke?

Because they can't fit their butts in the ashtray!

How do you stop a cow from mooing?

Use a moo-fler!

What did the beaver say to the tree?

"It's been good gnawing you!"

Two mice ran up the clock. The clock struck one and the other one got away with a minor injury!

Two horses were standing in a field. One says, "I'm so hungry, I could eat a horse!"

The other horse replies, "Moo!"

248

What do you get if you cross an elephant with a bird?

A gulp. It's like a swallow, only bigger!

How do you get milk from a polar bear?

Steal it from his fridge and run very fast!

What do you get if you cross a dog with a hippo?

A mud-hound!

Who do you call if a parrot falls off its perch?

A parrot-medic!

249

Why did the zookeeper separate the gnus?

Because he had good gnus and bad gnus!

What did the farmer give to the sick chicken.

Tweet-ment!

Ethan: "Our new dog is like a member of the family."

Craig: "I can see the resemblance!"

What kind of fish can't swim?

Dead ones!

What is large, grey and goes round and round?

An elephant stuck in a revolving door!

What sort of fish do you find in your shoe?

An eel!

What do you get if you cross a chicken with a cow?

Roost beef!

What do you call a sheep in a rainstorm?

A wet blanket!

Why are elephants wiser than chickens?

Ever heard of Kentucky Fried Elephant?

What did the chimp say when his sister had a baby?

"Well I'll be a monkey's uncle!"

What kind of bird lays electric eggs?

A battery hen!

What do you call a pig driving a car?

Road hog!

What do you call a pig with fleas?

Pork scratchings!

What happened to the ray when it met a Tiger shark?

It became an X-ray!

What do you get if you cross a flat fish with a bird?

Cheep-skate!

Why did the starfish blush?

Because it saw the ship's bottom!

What do you call a fish on the table?

A plaice-mat!

Which side of a chicken has the most feathers?

The outside!

What do you call a cow with a twitch?

Beef jerky!

What happened to the ship that sank in shark-infested water?

It came back with a skeleton crew!

Why are farmers cruel?

Because they pull the ears off corn!

What key won't open a door?

A turkey!

What did the mouse say when it broke its teeth?

"Hard cheese!"

What do you call the pink bits between a shark's teeth?

Slow swimmers!

What do you get if you cross a dog and a vegetable patch?

A jack brussel!

What do you call a rabbit on a diet?

Thinning hare!

What's green and fluffy?

A seasick kitten!

Why didn't the zebra like the sea?

There was something fishy about it!

What is brown and furry on the inside and white on the outside?

A rat sandwich!

Which hand would you use to grab a venomous snake?

Someone else's.

Where does a down-and-out octopus live?

On squid row!

What's worse than it raining cats and dogs?

Hailing taxis!

What do cows produce when it's hot?

Evaporated milk!

What monkey can fly?

A hot air baboon!

What kind of animal has four legs and can see just as well at both ends?

A gazelle with its eyes closed!

Why did the cow jump over the moon?

Because the farmer had cold hands!

Why don't owls mate when it's raining?

Because it's too wet to woo!

How do rats keep their breath fresh?

They use mouse-wash!

What do you get if you cross a hedgehog with a giraffe?

A long-necked toothbrush!

Why do polar bears have fur coats?

Because when they wore anoraks, the seals laughed at them!

How do chickens dance?

Chick-to-chick!

What do you call mad sea cow disease?

Manatee insanity!

Animals

What do you call a man with a hippo on his head?

Squashed!

What's green and hangs from trees?

Monkey snot!

How do you know that chickens do overtime?

Because they work around the cluck!

What day do fish hate?

Fry-day!

Why don't turkeys get invited to parties?

Because they use fowl language!

Did you hear about the wolf that ate the sheep?

He felt baaaaaaaaaaad!

Who goes into a tiger's den and comes out alive?

A tiger!

Why can't two elephants swim together?

They only have one pair of trunks between them!

Why did the crab get arrested?

He kept pinching things!

What do you call a bear in a monsoon?

A drizzly bear!

What do you call a whale that can't stop talking?

A blubber mouth!

Why do mice fall over when you cut them in half?

Because a mouse divided against itself cannot stand!

What did the baby chick say when he saw his mother sitting on an orange?

"Look what marma-laid!"

What do you call a mammoth who conducts an orchestra?

Tusk-anini!

What do you call a dog in the middle of a muddy path?

A mutt in a rut!

What is a bird in the hand worth?

I don't know, but it makes it hard to blow your nose!

How do you save a drowning rodent?

Mouse to mouse resuscitation!

What happens if you try to cross a lion with a goat?

You'll have to get a new goat!

What is black, white and flat?

A zebra that's been run over with a steamroller!

What has twelve legs, six ears, a foul smell and one eye?

Three blind mice and half a rotten fish!

You know what they say about a bird in the hand?

It poos on your wrist!

What did the rooster say when he stepped in a cow pat?

Cock-a-doodle-poo!

Animals

Mum: "Josh, please put the cat out again!"
Josh: "Why, is it on fire again?"

I just got a puppy for my little brother.
Sounds like a fair trade!

What's big and grey and protects you from the rain?
An umbrelle-phant!

Why did the turkey stop eating his dinner?
He was already stuffed!

Which animal needs oil?
A mouse, because it squeaks!

What's the best way to catch a fish?

Have someone throw one at you!

Where did the killer whale go to get his teeth fixed?

The orca-dontist!

What do you get if you cross a shark with a parrot?

A bird that talks your ear off!

What's black, white, black, white, black, white....

A zebra on a roundabout!

What happened when the monkey chased the banana?

The banana split!

What lives under the sea and bites all the fish?

A clamp-ire!

What did the fish say when it swam into the wall?

"Dam!"

Why did the fisherman throw peanut butter into the ocean?

To go with the jellyfish!

Why did the ocean roar?

Because it had crabs on its bottom!

Who eats its prey two by two?

Noah's shark!

Did you hear about the dog that ran 100 miles to get a stick?

It seems a bit far fetched!

If a fire hydrant has H2O on the inside, what does it have on the outside?

K9p!

What fish does a builder use?

A pneumatic krill!

Who lost a herd of elephants?

Big Bo Peep!

Sarah: "Why do you call your cat Rain?"

Molly: "He keeps leaving puddles everywhere!"

What do you call an elephant in an elevator?

Stuck!

Bird 1: "Wow, look how fast those planes can fly."

Bird 2: "you'd fly that fast too if your bum was on fire!"

What do you get if you cross a serpent with a trombone?

A snake in the brass!

What's a toad's favourite ballet?

Swamp Lake!

What do you call a pig with no eyes?

Pg!

What animal goes 'clip, clip'?

A horse hopping sideways!

Why did the parrot wear a raincoat?

So it could be poly-unsaturated!

Why did the chicken cross the road, roll in mud and cross back over again?

Because it was a dirty double-crosser!

What do you call a cow spying on another cow?

A steak out!

Why did the cow pat cross the road?

Because it was a stand-in!

What's white, has big ears and a trunk?

A mouse on vacation!

What's brown, has big ears and a trunk?

A mouse returning from vacation!

What do you get if you cross a kangaroo with an elephant?

Huge potholes all over Australia!

What do you call a monkey holding a bomb?

Ba-boom!

What do you call a goose who likes eating prunes?

A loose goose!

What do you give an elephant with an upset stomach?

Plenty of room!

What has four legs and flies?

A dead cow!

If I had eight hedgehogs in one hand and seven hedgehogs in the other, what would I have?

Big hands with lots of splinters!

Why are giraffes so slow to apologize?

It takes them a long time to swallow their pride!

How many sheep does it take to knit a sweater?

None, sheep can't knit!

What's black and white and red all over?

An embarrassed panda!

What do you get if you cross a rabbit with a kettle?

A hot cross bunny!

What do you get if you cross a hen with a guitar?

A chicken that plucks itself!

What's the best way to communicate with a fish?

Drop it a line!

Why does a stork lift one leg?

Because if it lifted both, it would fall over!

What do you call a crate full of ducks?

A box of quackers!

What happens when you put a goat in a blender?

You get a crazy mixed-up kid!

What goes black white, black white, black white, black white?

A penguin rolling down a hill!

What's black and white and goes, 'Ha, ha, ha'?

The penguin that pushed him!

Animals

Why does a monkey scratch itself?

Because he's the only one who knows where it itches!

What did one firefly say to the other when his light went out?

"Give me a push, my battery's dead!"

What's black and white and purple?

A zebra with a peg on its nose!

Why do lions eat raw meat?

Have you ever tried to teach one to cook?

What do you call a building full of pigs?

A sty-scraper!

273

What has two wings, two arms, two tails, three heads and eight legs?

A man on a horse holding a chicken!

What do you call a pig that took a plane?

Swine flu!

Two fish in a tank, one turns to the other and says, "Do you know how to drive this thing?"

What do you call a rhino who drinks too much?

A whino!

What's grey and moves faster than the speed of sound?

A jet propelled elephant!

Why don't ducks tell jokes when they're flying?

Because they'd quack up!

What do you call a stupid squid?

A squid-iot!

Man 1: "Your dog's been chasing a woman on a bicycle."

Man 2: "Don't be silly, my dog can't ride a bike!"

How do you tell one cat from another?

Look them up in a cat-alogue!

What do you call a cow with two legs?

Lean beef!

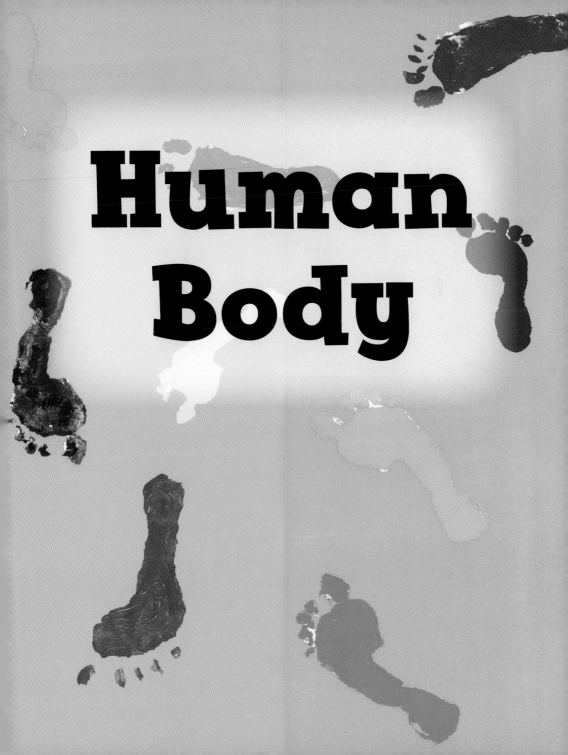

Human Body

Patient: "Doctor, doctor, I keep thinking I'm a toilet!"

Doctor: "I thought you were looking rather flushed!"

How can you cure a headache?
Put your head through the window and the pane will disappear!

Tom: "What do you clean your top teeth with?"
Josh: "A toothbrush?"
Tom: "And?"
Josh: "Toothpaste."
Tom: "And what about your bottom?"
Josh: "The same."
Tom: "Eurgh! That's disgusting, I use toilet paper!"

Why did the sword-swallower switch to pins and needles?

He needed to lose weight!

Did you hear about the plastic surgeon?

He sat by the fire and melted!

Patient: "Doctor, doctor, I've got a strawberry stuck up my bum."

Doctor: "I've got some cream for that!"

What do you get if someone hits you on the head with an axe?

A splitting headache!

What's bright red and stupid?
A blood clot!

How can you cure dandruff?
Cut off your head!

Patient: "Doctor, doctor, I'm scared. This is my first operation."

Doctor: "I know how you feel, it's my first one, too!"

What has a bottom at its top?
A leg! .

What should you do if your nose goes on strike?
Picket!

What do you say to a one-legged hitch hiker?

"Hop in!"

What do you call a judge with no thumbs?

Justice Fingers!

Lauren: "My beauty is timeless."

Jason: "Yes, it could stop clocks!"

What do surgeons do with their mistakes?

Bury them!

What has two legs but can't walk?

A pair of jeans!

What can you keep and give to someone else at the same time?
The flu!

When is it wrong to bury people in a graveyard?
When they're still alive!

Knock, knock.
Who's there?
Juliet.
Juliet who?
Juliet so many sausages she feels ill!

Patient: "Doctor, doctor, you've taken out my tonsils, my adenoids, my gall bladder, my varicose veins and my appendix, but I still don't feel well."
Doctor: "That's quite enough out of you!"

I never forget a face, but in your case I'll make an exception!

Patient: "Doctor, doctor, I'm at death's door!"
Doctor: "Don't worry, I'll pull you through!"

An old man and his wife were sitting in a library. The old man said, "I just let out a silent fart. What should I do?" His wife said, "Well for one thing you should change your hearing aid battery!"

Tom: "Our teacher has a sympathetic face."
Josh: "What do you mean?"
Tom: "People look at her and feel sympathy!"

What do you call a nun with a washing machine on her head?

Sister-Matic!

What happened to the boy who swallowed a torch?

He hiccupped with delight!

What man never gets his hair wet in the shower?

A bald one!

What do you call a woman with only one tooth?

Peg!

Sarah: "Why aren't you taking Jake to the prom? I thought you said it was love at first sight."

Lisa: "It was the second and third viewings that put me off!"

Patient: "Doctor, doctor, I keep thinking I'm a pool ball."

Doctor: "Get to the end of the queue!"

Did the native Americans hunt bear?

Not in the winter!

What do children and gardeners have in common?

They both have green fingers!

What does a boy do when a girl rolls her eyes at him?

Rolls them back!

Surgeon: "I'm afraid we have good news and bad news: the bad news is that we've had to take off both your feet. The good news is that the man in the next bed wants to buy your slippers!"

Knock, knock.

Who's there?

Ivor.

Ivor who?

Ivor a spot on my bum!

What kind of monster gets up your nose?

The bogey-man!

Patient: "Doctor, doctor, what does this X-ray of my head show?"

Doctor: "Unfortunately, nothing!"

Why did the crazy undertaker chop all his corpses into tiny bits?

He wanted them to rest in pieces!

287

Human Body

What should you do with rotten nails?

Save them in a nail file!

What has ears, but can't hear?

Corn!

Patient: "Doctor, doctor, my mind keeps wandering."

Doctor: "Don't worry – it's too weak to go very far!"

What happened when the girl found out her boyfriend had a wooden leg?

She broke it off!

Why did the thief saw his legs off?

He wanted to lie low!

What do you call a sleep-walking nun?

A roaming catholic!

Patient: "Doctor, doctor, I can't stop sneezing."

Doctor: "Don't worry - it's much achoo about nothing!"

What's the difference between a thermometer that goes up your bottom, and one that goes in your mouth?

The taste!

What did one tonsil say to the other?

"Get dressed. The doctor's taking us out tonight!"

What might you win if you lose ten kilos?

The Nobel-ly Prize!

Why did the sword-swallower swallow an umbrella?

He wanted to put something away for a rainy day!

Patient: Doctor, doctor, I've developed a double heart beat since my operation.

Doctor: Ah, so that's where my wristwatch went!

Where does an undertaker work?

In a box office!

How can you stop your nose running?

Stick out your foot and trip it up!

Tom: "This morning I put soap flakes in my brother's cornflakes."

Josh: "What happened?"

Tom: "He got so mad, he was foaming at the mouth!"

Patient: "Doctor, doctor, I keep breaking wind. Is there anything you can suggest?"

Doctor: "Yes, take up wind surfing!"

How do you know if someone has a glass eye?

It comes out in conversation!

Why did the sword-swallower only swallow half a sword?

He was having a mid-knife crisis!

Sarah: "Dad, there's a man with a beard at the door."

Dad: "Tell him I already have one!"

How do your teeth stay together?

Toothpaste!

What did one crash test dummy say to the other crash test dummy?

"Can I crash at your place tonight?"

Patient: "Doctor, doctor, I've swallowed a roll of film."

Doctor: "Sit in a darkened room and we'll see what develops!"

What did one bogey say to another?

"You think you're funny, but you're snot!"

Why were the Baker's hands brown and sticky?

Because he kneaded a poo!

Knock, knock.

Who's there?

Dishes.

Dishes who?

Dishes the way I talk now I've got false teeth!

Patient: "Doctor, doctor, every time I stand up I see Mickey and Minnie Mouse and every time I sit down I see Donald Duck and Goofy."

Doctor: "Don't worry, you're just having Disney spells!"

Why did the monster take his nose apart?

To see what made it run!

Did you hear the joke about the chiropodist?

It's kind of corny!

Patient: "Doctor, doctor, will my measles be gone by the weekend?"

Doctor: "I don't want to make any rash promises!"

What did the bald man say when he received a comb for his birthday?

"Thanks, I'll never part with it!"

295

Why did the angel go to the doctor?

She had harp failure!

How did the man feel after he got run over?

Tyred!

Patient: "Doctor, doctor, I feel like a piano."

Doctor: "I'd better make some notes!"

What do people with weak bladders and people who wear old stockings have in common?

They both get runs down their legs!

What do you call a lorry full of feet?

A toe truck!

What can you catch, but not throw?

Your breath!

Patient: "Doctor, doctor, I can't stop trembling."

Doctor: "I'll be with you in a couple of shakes!"

What happened to the thief who stole from the blood bank?

He got caught red handed!

Why did the undertaker's son not want to follow in his father's footsteps?

He thought it was a dead end job!

What grows between your nose and your chin?

Two-lips!

Josh: "Dad, how old are you?"

Dad: "41, but I don't look it do I?"

Josh: "No, you used to!"

Patient: "Doctor, doctor, my eyes keep falling out. Can you give me something to keep them in?"

Doctor: "How about this plastic bag?"

What do you call a lady with one leg shorter than the other?

Eileen!

Did you hear about the stupid couple that got frostbite at the drive-in movie?

They went to see 'Closed for Winter'!

Lauren: "Richard is off school because Sarah broke an arm."

Jason: "Well why is Richard off school if Sarah broke an arm?"

Lauren: "It was his arm she broke!"

Why did the secretary cut her fingers off?

So she could do short hand!

Patient: "Doctor, doctor, I just swallowed a bone."

Doctor: "Are you choking?"

Patient: "No, I'm being serious!"

Patient: "Doctor, doctor, I have a hoarse throat."

Doctor: "The resemblance doesn't stop there!"

How do you know if you're upside down?

Your nose runs and your feet smell!

Doctor: "I need to take your pulse."

Patient: "Haven't you got one of your own?"

Patient: "Doctor, doctor, I think I've been bitten by a vampire."

Doctor: "Drink this water."

Patient: "Will it make me better?"

Doctor: "No, but I want to see if your neck leaks!"

Craig: "What are you taking for that cough?"

Sarah: "How much will you give me for it?"

What stands in New York and sneezes all day?

The a-choo of liberty!

Human Body

How can you stop a head cold becoming a chest cold?

Tie a knot in your neck!

Knock, knock.
Who's there?
Watson.
Watson who?
Watson on your nose, it's gross!

Patient: "Doctor, doctor, I'm going bald, is there any cure?"

Doctor: "Yes, smear poo on your head every morning."

Patient: "And that will stop my hair falling out?"

Doctor: "No, but nobody will come near enough to you to notice you're bald!"

What does a dentist call her X-rays?

Tooth-pics!

Patient: "Doctor, doctor, I've got a terrible cough."

Doctor: "Then you should practice more!"

Tom: "If I had 30 pineapples in one hand and 30 pineapples in the other hand, what would I have?"

Josh: "Enormous hands!"

Bar of soap: "Sometimes I think I have the worst job in the world."

Toilet paper: "Think again!"

Human Body

How do you make
a Venetian blind?
Stick your finger
in his eye!

What can run,
but not walk?
Your nose!

Patient: "Doctor, doctor, I've got
strawberries growing out of my head."

Doctor: "Here's some cream for them!"

What has four legs,
but only one foot?
A bed!

Why are false teeth like stars?

They only come out at night!

What happened to the man who ate too much blue cheese?

He blew chunks!

How many people does it take to wallpaper a room?

Two, but only if they're thinly sliced!

How many psychiatrists does it take to change a light bulb?

Only one, but the light bulb has to really want to change!

What's the most musical part in your body?

Your nose because you can pick it and blow it!

What do werewolves eat to keep their teeth in good condition?

Dentists!

What do you give someone who has flat feet?

A foot pump!

Doctor: "You need new glasses."

Patient: "How do you know? I haven't told you what's wrong with me yet."

Doctor: "I could tell as soon as you walked in through the window!"

Why is your nose in the middle of your face?

Because it is the scenter!

Knock, knock.
Who's there?
Emma.
Emma who?
Emma 'fraid you have an ugly face!

Patient: "Doctor, doctor, I've lost my memory."
Doctor: "When did this happen?"
Patient: "When did what happen?"

How do you turn a normal scientist into a mad scientist?

Stamp on his feet!

Mum: "Tom, did you take a bath?"

Tom: "Why? Is one missing?"

Patient: "Doctor, doctor, I swallowed my harmonica."

Doctor: "Be thankful you don't play the piano!"

Craig: "My sister should've been born in the Dark Ages."

James: "Why?"

Craig: "She looks awful in daylight!"

What's the best way to stop acid indigestion?

Don't drink acid!

Molly: "My doctor said I should drink some tea after a hot bath."

Sarah: "Did it work?"

Molly: "I haven't finished drinking the bath yet!"

What happened to the burglar who fell into a cement mixer?

He became a hardened criminal!

What did the surgeon say when he finished the operation?

"That's enough out of you!"

What kind of bandages do people wear after heart surgery?

Ticker tape!

Patient: "Doctor, doctor, my nose is running."

Doctor: "Then get after it quick!"

Patient: "Doctor, doctor, when I press with my finger here... it hurts, and here... it hurts, and here... and here... What do you think is wrong with me?"

Doctor: "You have a broken finger!"

What's a chiropodist's favourite song?

There's no business like toe business!

Patient: "Doctor, doctor, I keep hearing a ringing in my ears?"

Doctor: "Where did you expect to hear it?"

Patient: "Doctor, doctor, can you give me some aspirin and some glue?"

Doctor: "Why?"

Patient: "I have a splitting headache!"

Did you hear about the plastic surgeon?

He went on holiday to Spain and melted!

311

Did you hear the joke about the cesspit?

It takes a while to sink in!

What do you call a girl who never uses a tissue?

Green-sleeves!

Mum: "I think our daughter got her brains from me."

Dad: "She must have, because I've still got mine!"

How many knees do you have?

Four: your right knee, your left knee and two kidneys!

What do you find up a clean nose?

Fingerprints!

How long does it take to learn to roller skate?

About 100 sittings!

What do you call a woman with a sinking ship on her head?

Mandy Lifeboats!

Did you hear about the woman who said she had the face of a 16 year old?

The police made her give it back!

Patient: "Doctor, doctor, I need something for my kidneys."

Doctor: "Here's a pound of steak - make yourself a pie!

Tom: "I saw a sign earlier that made me wet myself."

Josh: "What did it say?"

Tom: "Toilet closed!"

Did you hear about the dentist who became a brain surgeon?

His drill slipped!

My sister is so keen on road safety that she always wears white at night. Although she did get run over by a snow plough recently!

What do you call a man with a chest cold?

Fleming!

What kind of monster can sit on your finger?

The bogey-man!

Doctor: "Now, tell me again how you burned both of your ears?"

Patient: "Well I was ironing when the phone rang and I picked up the iron and put that to my ear by mistake."

Doctor: "But how did you burn both ears?"

Patient: "The phone rang again!"

Patient: "Doctor, doctor, I have chronic diarrhea"

Doctor: "Yes, it runs in the family!"

Food

What's the Pied Piper's preferred dinner?

Rat-atouie!

What's the difference between cabbage and bogies?

Kids like to eat bogies!

What's the difference between a fried egg and pea soup?

You can fry an egg, but you can't pea soup!

Peter: "What are you going to do with all that manure?

John: "I'm going to put it on my strawberries."

Peter: "Yuck! I put sugar and cream on mine!"

318

What vegetable can you find in the toilet?

A leek!

What nut can you find in a toilet?

A peanut!

What's yellow and dangerous?

Shark-infested custard!

What's the difference between a sausage roll and a dead rat?

I don't know.

Then I'll eat the sausage roll and you can have the dead rat!

Why are fried onions like a photocopier?

They keep repeating themselves!

What do zombies eat with bread and cheese?

Pickled organs!

Why were the peppers red?

They saw the salad dressing!

Why were the tomatoes red?

Because the greengrocer told them rude stories!

What did the vegetarian, man-eating tiger eat?

Swedes!

What's a mushroom?

The school dining hall!

What do you get if you cross a pig with a zebra?

Striped bacon!

What do you get if you cross a birthday cake with a tin of baked beans?

A cake that blows out its own candles!

What soup do witches eat?

Scream of chicken!

Why did Gary eat little bits of metal all day?

It was his staple diet!

How can you stop fish going bad on Monday?

Eat it on Sunday!

What's yellow, brown and hairy?

Cheese on toast dropped on the carpet!

What did the sausage say as it was about to be put on a skewer?

"Oh spear me, spear me!"

What do you get if you cross a dog with an omelet?

Pooched eggs!

What did one onion say to the other?

"How did we get into this pickle?"

What fish tastes good with ice cream?

Jelly-fish!

I had a dream I ate a giant marshmallow last night...

... I woke up without a pillow!

Patient: "Doctor, doctor, I keep thinking I'm a fruitcake."

Doctor: "What's got into you?"

Patient: "Raisins, cherries, flour..."

Why do sausages have such bad manners?

They spit in the frying pan!

Sarah was feeling seasick on her cruise when the waiter asked if she would like some lunch.

"No thanks," she replied, "just throw it overboard and save me the trouble!"

Patient: "Doctor, doctor, I've got a carrot growing out of my ear."

Doctor: "That's amazing."

Patient: "I know, I planted potatoes in there!"

Patient: "Doctor, doctor, I feel like an apple."

Doctor: "We must get to the core of this!"

What do you call a woman who has toast on her head?

Marge!

Patient: "Doctor, doctor, every time I drink hot chocolate I get a sharp pain in my eye."

Doctor: "Try taking the spoon out before you drink it!"

325

Patient: "Doctor, doctor, I feel like an apple."
Doctor: "Well come closer, I don't bite!"

"Waiter, there's a fly in my soup!"
"Not to worry sir, the spider in your salad will get it!"

What's round, white, stinky and giggly?
A tickled onion!

Patient: "Doctor, doctor, I feel like a raspberry."
Doctor: "Well I can see you're in a jam!"

What do you call cheese that isn't yours?

Nacho cheese!

"Waiter, your thumb is in my soup!"

"Don't worry sir, it's not hot!"

What's the definition of a balanced diet?

The same amount of cookies in each hand!

Why did the cookie go to the doctor?

It felt crumby!

What do you give a badly injured lemon?

Lemon-aid!

What's thick, yellow and grows on trees?

A stupid banana!

Patient: "Doctor, doctor, I think I've got jelly in my ear."

Doctor: "You're just a trifle deaf!"

"Waiter, this egg is rotten!"

"Don't blame me, I only laid the table!"

Patient: "Doctor, doctor, sometimes I think I'm an onion, and sometimes a beetroot."

Doctor: "I can see you're in a pickle!"

What is a shark's dessert of choice?

Jellyfish!

"Waiter, there's a fly on my steak."

"That's because they seem to be attracted to rotting meat!"

"Waiter, there's a spider in my soup."

"It must have eaten the fly!"

How do you make a banana shake?

Sneak up on it and scream!

Did you hear about the carrot that died?

There was a big turn-up at the funeral!

How did the beans affect Billy's intestines?

They rectum!

"Waiter, there's a fly in my soup."

"No sir, that's a cockroach, the fly is on your role!"

"Waiter, this soup tastes funny!"

"Then why aren't you laughing?"

Patient: "Doctor, doctor, what's wrong with me?"

Doctor: "Well, you have sweetcorn up your nose and a sausage in your ear. I'd say you're not eating right!"

What's a ghost's choice of meal?

Goulash!

"Waiter, there's a cockroach in my soup."

"Sorry, Sir, all out of flies!"

What do skeletons say to each other before eating a meal?

"Bone-appetite!"

What did one teddy bear say to the other teddy bear when they were offered dessert?

"No thanks, I'm stuffed!"

How did the jury find the hamburger?

Grill-ty as charred!

How do gossipy burgers spend their time?

They chew the fat!

"Waiter, there's a fly in my soup."

"Don't worry, they don't drink much!"

What did the mayonnaise say when the fridge door opened?

"Close the door, I'm dressing!"

What's worse than finding a slug in your apple?

Finding half a slug in your apple!

What do you call a girl with sausages on her head?

Barbie!

"Waiter, what's this fly doing on my ice cream?"

"It looks like he's learning to ski!"

What nuts are always covered in bogies?

Cashews!

What's the scariest fruit?

A Boo-nana!

What's a ghost's preferred jelly?

Lemon and Slime!

What's the rudest vegetable?

A pea!

"Waiter, there's a huge bug in my soup!"

"Be quiet, Sir, everyone will want one!"

What does a termite eat for breakfast?

Oak-meal!

"Waiter, how did this fly get in my soup?"

"It flew!"

What do devils drink?

Demon-ade!

What's a vampire's preferred fruit?

Blood Orange!

How do you make a swiss roll?

Push him down a hill!

Mum: "Haven't you finished filling the salt shaker yet?"

Matt: "Not yet, it's really hard to get the salt through all those little holes!"

335

What's yellow and stupid?

Thick custard!

What do monsters call knights in armor?

Tinned food!

Why did the man drown in his muesli?

He was pulled under by a strong currant!

What does a cannibal call the phone book?

The takeaway menu!

"Waiter, why is your thumb on my steak?"

"I don't want to drop it again!"

What's the most musical part of a turkey?

The drumstick!

Did you hear about the man who put his false teeth in backwards?

He ate himself!

A family of three tomatoes were walking in town one day when the baby tomato started to fall behind. Big daddy tomato walked back to baby tomato, stomped on her and said, "Ketchup!"

How do monsters like their eggs on a morning?

Terri-fried!

Why do idiots eat biscuits?

Because they're crackers!

What do zombies eat for breakfast?

Dreaded wheat!

Why did the monster trample all over his cornflakes?

He was a cereal killer!

"Waiter, do you have frogs' legs?"

"How dare you! I've always walked like this!"

Did you hear about the cannibal who was late for lunch?

He was given the cold shoulder!

What did the grape do when the elephant sat on it?

Let out a little wine!

Which martial artist lives in a pod?

Bruce Pea!

What do witches like to eat as a summer time treat?

Leeches and cream!

What do you get if you cross a biscuit with a monster?

Crumbs!

Why do pixies eat their food so quickly?

Because they're always goblin!

What do you get if you cross a monster with peanut butter?

A monster that sticks to the roof of your mouth!

How do you make a monster float?

Take two scoops of ice-cream, a glass of cola and add one monster!

What does Dracula have for breakfast?

Ready-neck!

What's purple and hums?

A rotten plum!

Did you hear about the monster who went on a crash diet?

He wrecked three cars and a bus!

What do monsters eat for dessert?

Boo-berry pie!

"Waiter, there's a small insect in my soup."

"My apologies sir, I shall fetch you a larger one!"

What is yellow and white and throws itself off the edge of the table?

A lemming meringue!

What's the difference between an interfering neighbor and a naked apple?

One is rude and nosy.
The other is nude and rosy!

On which day do monsters eat people?

Chews-day!

What do hedgehogs enjoy as an afternoon snack?

Prickled onions!

What do you get from naughty cows?

Bad milk!

What's the difference between Frankenstein's monster and boiled potatoes?

You can't mash Frankenstein's monster!

342

How do you save lamb chops from drowning?

Put them in gravy boats!

Where can you learn to make ice-cream?

At sundae school!

Why should you stay calm when meeting a cannibal?

Otherwise you would be in a stew!

"Waiter, is there any soup on the menu?"

"No sir, I wiped it all off!"

343

"Mummy, Mummy,
I don't like Daddy."

"Well just eat your
salad then!"

What vegetable
should you never
have on a boat?

A leek!

"Waiter, what is this fly
doing in my soup?"

"It looks like the backstroke sir!"

What do they have for lunch
at Monster School?

Human beans, boiled legs, pickled
bunions and eyes-cream!

Why were there screams coming from the kitchen?

The cook was beating the eggs!

What's pink and dangerous?

A six month old sausage!

What cake gives you an electric shock?

A current bun!

Where do ghosts buy their food?

At the ghost-ery store!

Do zombies eat popcorn with their fingers?

No, they eat the fingers separately!

"Waiter, this is disgusting, I can't eat it! Call the manager."

"It's no use. He won't eat it either!"

Why wasn't there any food left after the monster party?

Because everyone was a goblin!

What do you call a nut with a cold?

Ca-shew!

Did you hear about the farmer who ploughed his field with a steamroller?

He wanted to grow mashed potatoes!

What are the two things you won't eat for lunch?

Breakfast and dinner!

What would you get if you crossed a werewolf with a dozen eggs?

A very hairy omelette!

Customer: "Waiter, what are today's soups?"

Waiter: "Chicken soup, and pea soup."

Customer: "I'll have a chicken soup."

Waiter: "One chicken soup."

Customer: "No wait, I've changed my mind. Hold the chicken and make it pea."

Waiter: "I'll do my best, Sir!"

What did one snowman say to the other?

"Can you smell carrots?"

What's brown, hairy and coughs?

A coconut with a cold!

How do you make hard-boiled eggs?

Give your chickens boiling water!

How do you make an orange laugh?

Tickle its navel!

What did one strawberry say to the other?

"If you'd listened to me, we wouldn't be in this jam!"

What food can defend itself?

Kung-food!

What happened when the Swede died?

There was a huge turnip at its funeral!

Why shouldn't you eat on an empty stomach?

You should eat on a plate!

Is it OK to eat with your fingers?

No, you should eat your fingers separately!

"Stop reaching over the table like that, haven't you got a tongue?"

"Yes, but my arm's longer!"

Which fruit did Beethoven like to eat the most.

Ba-na-na-na, ba-na-na-na!

What do you call a monkey on top of a cake?

A marzipan-zee!

What is the most unreliable vegetable?

A fickle onion!

Tom: "My mum eats like a bird?"
Josh: "You mean she hardly eats anything?"
Tom: "No, she eats slugs and worms!"

What do you call a rotten hot dog?

A rank-furter!

What's fat, purple and wobbles?

A fat, purple jelly monster!

Josh: "My dad went on a crash diet this week."

Tom: "Oh, is that why he looks like a wreck?"

"Waiter, I'd like to swap my German sausage for a sea bird."

"Well that would be a tern for the wurst!"

What kind of key opens a banana?

A monkey!

What's the rear entrance to a cafeteria called?

A bacteria!

What do you call two banana peels?

A pair of slippers!

Mum: "If you eat any more cake you'll burst."

Adam: "OK, just pass the cake and run for cover!"

Josh: "Does ham grow on trees?"

Dad: "Of course not."

Josh: "Well, what's an ambush then?"

What do you call a peeled potato?

A spuddy in the nuddy!

If I bought 100 buns for 50 cents, what would each bun be?

Stale!

What's the dumbest fish in the school called?

Dinner!

My mum's gravy is so thick, when you stir it the house spins around!

"Waiter, this meal's half cold."
"Well eat the other half then!"

Mum: "Why is your sister crying?"

Craig: "Because I won't give her one of my chips."

Mum: "Well, what has she done with her own chips?"

Craig: "She cried when I ate them, too!"

What do you get if you cross a computer with a banana skin?

A slipped disc!

What's Australia's most popular drink?

Coca-Koala!

Why is Europe like a frying pan?

Because it has Greece at the bottom!

What do school cheese and the school cook's nose have in common?

They both smell and they're both runny!

There are two muffins in an oven, one turns to the other and says, "Blimey it's hot in here."

The other muffin says, "Oh, my God! A talking muffin!"

Why should you be worried if you eat bad food in Germany?

Because the wurst is yet to come!

What's tall, Italian and covered in pepperoni?

The leaning tower of pizza!

If you take a pie and eat three quarters, what are you left with?

Stomach-ache!

Craig: "Ask your brother what worms taste like."

Tom: "Why, how would he know?"

Craig: "Because there was one in that apple I just gave to him!"

How do you make an egg roll?

Push it!

What's small, round, black and runs on batteries?

An electric currant!

Why did the orange only get halfway across the road?

It ran out of juice!

"Waiter, these peas are as hard as bullets."

"Let me taste... well, they seem soft enough to me."

"That's because I've been chewing them for the last ten minutes!"

What do hedgehogs like on their sandwiches?

Cheese and prickle!

When is a detective mystery like an egg?

When you crack it!

What's cold and green and has a cherry on top?

A snot sundae!

What's white on the outside, green on the inside and hops?

A frog sandwich!

Are caterpillars good to eat?

Of course not, why?

Because there was one in your salad, and now there's not!

What's grey and powdery?

Instant elephant mix!

Have you heard the joke about the watermelon?

It's pitiful!

Tom: "What does your dad put on his carrots?"

Josh: "Cow manure."

Tom: "I prefer a little butter!"

How do you mop up golden syrup?

With treacle sponge!

Cannibal Mother: "Go get some salt, pepper and some plates."

Cannibal son: "But why?"

Cannibal Mother: "Because your sister's just fallen on the BBQ!"

Food

How did the man feel after eating a whole goose?

He felt pretty down!

What shoots stuffing across the room?

A turkey fart!

What do burps and kitchens have in common?

The both smell like dinner!

What did the elephant say to the orange?

"Let's play squash!"

What do you get when you mix tacos and a person who isn't feeling so good?

I don't know, but you're standing in it!

What do you get from a pampered cow?

Spoiled milk!

Why did the ham go to the doctor?

It wanted to be cured!

What's sugary on the outside and green on the inside?

A snot-filled donut!

What's worse than eating fresh vomit pie?

Eating two-day old vomit pie!

What happened to the butcher who sat on the meat slicer?

He got behind in his deliveries!

What's green, lumpy and comes in small pots?

Yogurt that's gone bad!

What do you get if a budgie flies into a blender?

Shredded-tweet!

Why did the coffee taste like mud?

Because it was only ground this morning!

What's green, brown and slimy, and comes out of your nose?

Chocolate milk after a good joke!

Did you hear about the fight in the chip shop?

Two fish got battered!

What pudding do cats like best?

Mice-pudding!

What's red, green, yellow and orange and wears boxing gloves?

A fruit punch!

What do you call a raspberry that's been run over?

A traffic jam!

Why did the donut go to the dentist?

To get a jam filling!

What's yellow and swings from cake to cake?

Tarz-ipan!

Why did the baker work so hard?

He kneaded the dough!

What do you get if you cross a biscuit with a tuxedo?

A smart cookie!

What food do cannibals like best?

Baked beings!

What do you get if you eat onions and baked beans?

Tear gas!

What do you get if you put honey on a chair?

Sticky buns!

What did one plate say to another?

Lunch is on me!

What do skeletons order from the butcher's?

Spare ribs!

What do ghosts put on their bagels?

Scream cheese!

Why is it a bad idea to write on an empty stomach?

Because it's much easier to write on paper!

Space

Patient: "Doctor, doctor, I keep seeing green aliens with five eyes and three legs."

Doctor: "Have you seen a psychiatrist?"

Patient: "No just green aliens with five eyes and three legs!"

What's an alien's choice of snack?

A Milky Way!

What did one alien plant say to the other?

"Take me to your weeder!"

What did E.T.'s mum say when he returned home?

"Where on earth have you been?"

Space

Where do astronauts leave their spaceships?

At parking meteors!

What do you call a crazy spaceman?

An astro-nut!

How do you get a baby alien to sleep?

Rocket!

Why did the cow go into space?

He wanted to see the mooooon!

What do you call a wizard from space?

A flying sorcerer!

How did Darth Vader know what Luke Skywalker was getting for Christmas?

He felt his presents!

What do aliens play with their friends?

Moon-opoly!

How do you address an angry looking alien with a ray gun?

Very politely!

If Martians live on Mars and Venusians live on Venus, who lives on Pluto?

Fleas!

Did you hear about the man who was captured by extra-terrestrial teddy bears?

He had a close encounter of the furred kind!

Why was the alien dog so itchy?

He had luna-tics!

What's green and goes 'Beep, beep'?

An alien in a traffic jam!

Can you destroy a Dalek by throwing eggs at him?

Of course, he'd be eggs-terminated!

Space

How does an alien count to 23?

On its fingers!

What alien has the best hearing?

The eeriest!

What did the martian say to the gas pump?

"Take your fingers out of your ears when I'm talking to you!"

What do you call an overweight alien?

An extra-cholesterol!

What do you call an alien with no eyes?

Alan!

Which sweets do aliens like best?

Martian-mallows!

Why should you never insult an alien?

You might hurt its feelers!

Why do aliens keep flying past Peter Pan's house?

Because it says 'Never Never Land'!

How did the rocket lose its job?

It got fired!

What cartoons do Martians watch?

Lunar Tunes!

Knock, knock.

Who's there?

Olive.

Olive who?

Olive in a flying saucer.

If an athlete gets athlete's foot, what does an astronaut get?

Missile-toe!

Why did the aliens get thrown out of the hotel?

They were flying the saucers!

Space

Why are aliens green?

Because they forgot to take their travel-sickness tablets!

What sort of star is dangerous?

A shooting star.

What is E.T. short for?

He has little legs!

What's Dracula's preferred sci-fi movie?

The Vampire Strikes Back!

What has eight legs and flies through space?

An unidentified flying octopus!

375

What's green on the inside, but grey on the outside and has a big trunk?

An alien disguised as an elephant!

What do aliens wear to weddings?

Space suits!

What sci-fi film is about an angry referee?

The Umpire Strikes Back!

Mum alien: "Don't eat that uranium."
Little alien: "Why not?"
Mum alien: "You'll get atomic-ache!"

What do you call an alien spaceship with broken air-conditioning?

A frying saucer!

What's green, wrinkly and has no teeth?

An alien grandad!

What's green and hairy?

An alien with a beard!

Why did Captain Kirk go into the ladies toilet?

To boldly go where no man has been before!

Why is lightning so badly behaved?

It doesn't know how to conduct itself!

What part of the keyboard do aliens like best?

The space bar!

Knock, knock.

Who's there?

Ann.

Ann who?

Ann Droid!

Did you hear about the alien with five legs?

His jeans fit him like a glove!

378

What sea is in space?

The galax-sea!

How do you know when the moon isn't hungry?

When it's full!

How can you tell when a robot is mad?

He goes screwy!

What did the robot eat for a light snack?

A 100-watt light bulb!

Why don't astronauts get hungry after being blasted into space?

Because they've just had a big launch!

What does an astronaut do when he gets angry?

He blasts off!

What kind of saddle do you put on a space horse?

A saddle-lite!

What is green, has two heads, three arms, five feet and six eyes?

An alien with spare parts!

380

Why is Saturn called Saturn?

Because it has a nice ring to it!

How does the solar system keep its trousers up?

With an asteroid belt!

What do you call an alien star ship that drips water and bogeys?

A crying saucer!

Where do aliens drink beer?

At a mars bar!

Knock, knock.

Who's there?

Armageddon.

Armageddon who?

Armageddon out of here, the aliens have landed!

Why couldn't the astronaut book a room on the moon?

Because it was full!

What should you do if you come across a blue alien?

Tell him a joke!

What did the alien win in a raffle?

The constellation prize!

How did the astronaut serve drinks?

In sun-glasses!

What do you call a Jedi teacher who sits on the floor cross legged?

Yoga!

Why are aliens great gardeners?

They have green fingers!

How does an alien shave?

With a laser blade!

Doctor Who has a new range of herbs and spices out.

Well, he is a thyme lord!

What do you get if you cross a Jedi teacher with a bear?

Yoda Bear!

What do you call a planet full of nasty aliens?

A waste of space!

How do you get 33 little aliens into your fridge?

Open the door!

Why do spacemen wear bullet proof vests?

Because of all the shooting stars!

Knock, knock.
Who's There?
Art.
Art Who?
R2-D2!

**Why did
the spaceman
go to the
optician?**
He had stars in
his eyes!

**Why was
the space robot
so silly?**
It had a screw
loose!

**What happened
when Anakin
threw moon
dust at Jar
Jar Binks?**
Jar Jar Blinked!

Why wouldn't you want Saturn to have a bath at your house?

He'd leave a filthy ring around the tub!

What do space monsters eat for a light snack?

Space-chips!

What do you get if you cross a Martian with a golf score?

A little green bogey!

If a meteor hits earth we call it a meteorite. What do we call the ones that miss?

Meteor-ongs!

386